THE HILLS OF SOUTHERN ENGLAND

Hills of England series

THE HILLS OF SOUTHERN ENGLAND

A Guide to Summits Under 20,00ft

ALASDAIR DIBB

MAINSTREAM PUBLISHING

EDINBURGH AND LONDON

For my mother and father

First published in Great Britain in 2002 by
MAINSTREAM PUBLISHING COMPANY
(EDINBURGH) LTD
7 Albany Street
Edinburgh EH1 3UG

ISBN 1 84018 536 8

A catalogue record for this book is available
from the British Library

Typeset in AGaramond
Printed and bound in Great Britain by Creative Print Design Wales

Advice to Readers

This guidebook has been carefully researched and prepared. However, whilst it is, to the best of the author's knowledge, accurate at the time of writing, paths, rights of way and access agreements are liable to change. Readers are advised to check locally before walking if in doubt. Neither the author nor publishers accept any liability for any disputes, accidents and damages arising from following any of the routes described in this book.

'There is a freedom in this vastness, these open downs, which far surpasses the most picturesque of landscapes . . . it is an almost prairie-like solitude.'

Richard Jefferies writing about the Wiltshire Downs (1877)

Contents

Acknowledgements

Whilst writing this book, I have received help and support from many people to whom I am indebted. I must thank Colin Dibb and Hazel Mackintosh for their company whilst walking and checking the routes, as well as investigating alternatives through rough and tough terrain. In addition, they have both, together with Christina Skaife and my editor, Ailsa Bathgate, given much time to reading through the typescript and made many helpful and useful suggestions that are all very much appreciated.

Writing this book would have been much more difficult if a published list of the relevant hills had not been available. Therefore, I would like to thank Alan Dawson, who wrote the original list, and all the others who have made suggestions that have prompted amendments to it. I would also like to thank Dr C.M. Huntley, Clerk of the List of Munroists for the Scottish Mountaineering Club, for providing me with up-to-date statistics on the number of Munroists. My thanks are also due to Edward Denne and Michael Ellis of Kent County Council for their help regarding rights-of-way closures on Cheriton Hill during the foot-and-mouth crisis. I must also thank Samantha Pentelow of Bodmin Tourist Information Centre for her research regarding the Rough Tor memorial on Brown Willy (Section 1).

I would like once again to thank Mary Philip for her advice regarding lead smelting, given whilst I was writing *England's Highest Peaks*. That material has now also been incorporated into this book as part of Section 2. I would also like to thank the following for their useful pieces of advice and encouragement: in no particular order, Susan Antal, Amelia Withers, Catherine Stevenson, Kathryn Smith, Richard Stebbings, Edward Humphreys, Rachel Firscht, Rebecca Eadie, Kate Seymour, Malcolm Rimmington, Hannah Barnett, Martin Oliver, Paul Morgan-Russell, Jamie Parmenter, Martin Nancekievill, Sam Ellis, Daniel Mason, Paul Mercer, Alan Roberts, Nick Kyte, Patrick Keddie, Helen Myers, Natalie MacDonald, Catherine Wise and anybody else who I may have unintentionally overlooked.

Finally, from the wild moors of the south-west to the sweeping whalebacks of the Downs, I hope that this book can help to introduce and encourage people to come and visit and walk in one of the most beautiful parts of Britain.

Alasdair Dibb
Tilehurst, Summer 2001

Introduction

Watch Croft, on the Land's End peninsula, is the most westerly hill on the British mainland; Cheriton Hill near Folkestone is the most easterly. In between these two, at the extremes of southern England, there are a further 35 distinct summits from Brighstone Down on the Isle of Wight to Bredon Hill on the northern edge of the Cotswolds near Evesham. In amongst them, there are thick pinewoods, curving downland crests, heather heaths, gnarled granite moors and spectacular coastlines. The hill landscapes of southern England have a little bit of everything: wilderness, rough uplands and pastoral farmlands. It is a special landscape, tame yet wild, and this book guides the walker to all of its most prominent summits.

All my life, I have lived on the top of a small hill that separates the valleys of the Thames and the Kennet to the west of Reading. From the village of Tilehurst, I can look northwards across the Thames Valley to the steep wooded southern slopes of the Chilterns. Westwards, the Pang Valley climbs slowly up the dipslope of the North Wessex Downs. Both of these areas are counted as 'Areas of Outstanding Natural Beauty' (AONBs).

In fact, this book takes the walker to 17 'Areas of Outstanding Natural Beauty', from Cornwall, through the Tamar Valley, Quantock Hills, Blackdown Hills, Mendip Hills, West Devon, East Dorset, Cranborne Chase and West Wiltshire Downs, North Wessex Downs, Chilterns, Isle of Wight, East Hampshire Downs, Sussex Downs, High Weald, Surrey Hills and Kent Downs to the Cotswolds – as well as the National Park of Exmoor (the South Downs are soon to be made a National Park). These count as exactly half of the 'Areas of Outstanding Natural Beauty' in the whole of England. The area under consideration, however, does not cover anywhere near half of England.

If this is the case, why then has southern England got such a reputation for having dull and uninspiring scenery compared to other parts of Britain? Well, I think I can answer this question. Despite living here for all my life, until a few years ago I always thought it was a fairly boring place.

I started climbing the hills as a means of getting fit for climbing in the Lake District, Scotland and further afield. However, although I had previously travelled extensively across the region, I suddenly began to realise the beauty that I had missed in the past.

The trouble is that the main roads tend to take the duller routes across the landscape and it is not until one gets off the busy roads, or better still goes walking, that the true beauty of the area is discovered. The most hardened summit baggers, for whom reaching a summit is simply another tick on their seemingly endless list, drive to all the summits of the south-east and see them as easy conquests. Unsurprisingly, in their quick dash to the top and back, they miss out on the best features, the hidden combes, the silent woodlands where the bluebells grow and the murmuring brooks. For them, the hills are simply the highest point of another road, or, perhaps more accurately, their ascent may be described as a trip to a car park and a short walk that is all over, with a bit of luck, in about five minutes flat. Is it surprising, therefore, that such people consider the hills of southern England to be boring?

I once met a man who claimed to have climbed 13 separate hills in a day. When pushed, it transpired that he had driven to the summits. Would it not be more accurate then to say that his car had done the climbing? Well, I certainly think so. Unless you actually climb the hills, it is impossible to appreciate their structure and dominance in the landscape. Without this perspective some merely turn into dull bumps – the steep slopes and towering escarpments are, in some cases, hidden by distance or vegetation. Having climbed all of these hills, there is not one that I would hesitate to recommend. I honestly believe that some of the summit baggers are missing so much, probably without even realising it. Outside the towns and away from the endless congested ribbons of tarmac there is beauty. In fact, I believe this is an area as beautiful as any other landscape in Britain. The Scottish Highlands may be wild and grand but in southern England there is a different kind of beauty, which is just as, and perhaps even more, mesmerising.

So, what makes a hill or even a mountain? It may sound like a simple question but it is one that has perplexed many climbers for at least a hundred years. In 1891, Sir Hugh Munro published the first 'list' of hills, including all the summits in Scotland above 3,000ft (914m), which he considered to be separate and, today, the majority of British hills and mountains have been included in some list or another. The publication of Alan Dawson's list of his so-called 'Marilyns' in 1992 meant that all the summits which rise more than 492ft (150m) from their surrounding landscape have been listed, although all the individual lists are remarkably different.

The way in which the lists differ is in their definition of what makes any given summit separate from another. Sir Hugh Munro made a personal decision but since then, the majority of authors have come up with at least one criterion to define the summits on their list. John Rooke Corbett was the first to do this when compiling his list of the Scottish mountains between 2,500ft (762m) and 3,000ft (914m) in altitude. He said that each summit on his list must have a drop of at least 500ft (152m) on all sides to detach it from a neighbouring peak. Later lists also adopted this criterion, including Fiona Graham's list of the Scottish summits between 2,000ft (610m) and 2,500ft (762m) in height and Alan Dawson's list of the 'relative hills' of Britain.

In southern England, it is Dawson's concept of relative height that is most appropriate to use when defining a hill. Although the relief of southern England rarely reaches any massive height, many of its hills are very high *relative* to their surroundings. Take this example: the summit of Aiguillette des Posettes in the French Alps is, at 7,215ft (2,199m) above sea level, 2,805ft (855m) higher than Britain's highest mountain, Ben Nevis. Despite this, however, it stands only 2,293ft (791m) above the village of Le Tour at its foot and 2,034ft (620m) of this height can be gained by the Col de Balme cable car.

From this perspective, therefore, it is no higher than the summits of many English mountains with respect to the valley levels at their bases. Compared to its nearby neighbour Mont Blanc, whose summit attains the dizzy height of 15,771ft (4,807m) above sea level, Aiguillette des Posettes is a mere tiddler. We could start to compare Mont Blanc with Mount Everest at 29,028ft (8,848m) but this would make little sense because, as anyone who has visited the town of Chamonix knows, Mont Blanc is massive. It towers high above the town and to describe it as a low and incidental summit is ridiculous. But, compared to Everest, Mont Blanc is low and incidental. The concept of absolute height is, therefore, ridiculous; we should, instead, talk in terms of relative height.

It is a fact that many of the hills of southern England *are* relatively high compared to their surrounding landscape. With valleys and vales little more than a few hundred feet above sea level at most, a summit that is 1,000ft (300m) in altitude, or even 700ft (210m) can appear to be massively high and the walker feels a great sense of elevation on reaching it. From personal experience, this sense of elevation is greater than is felt on many British mountains.

If the concept of relative height is taken to define a hill there is one remaining question: what quantity of relative height is most appropriate? Well, the figure of 500ft (152m) is most traditionally used and with good cause too. When studying two neighbouring summits from a nearby peak, a drop of 500ft (152m) is, in my opinion, about the correct height to define them as truly separate. It is generally agreed that a mountain is a summit above 2,000ft (610m). Thus, a hill is defined as a summit between 492ft (150m) – to follow the metric measures now used on maps – and 2,000ft (610m) in altitude, provided it is separated from any higher summit by a descent of at least 492ft (150m).

This is the concept that Alan Dawson used to write his list of 'Marilyns' in 1992. Dawson's extensive table covers the whole of Britain, giving a total of 1,552 summits. Of these, 179 are in England (37 in southern England) and 5 on the Isle of Man. A total of 50 in England and 1 on the Isle of Man exceed the height of 2,000ft (610m). Dawson's tables are published in his book *The Relative Hills of Britain* (see Further Reading).

As shown on the map in figure 1, the hills of England can be split into three convenient sections. This book, the first in a series of three, details the 37 hills between 492ft (150m) and 2,000ft (610m) in altitude that lie in southern England. In total, the other two books and *England's Highest Peaks* cover all the separate hills and mountains of England as defined by a descent of 492ft (150m) on all sides.

The Hills of England

Volume 1: Southern England includes the Cornish Hills, Exmoor, Quantocks, Mendips, Blackdown Hills, Wessex Downs, Isle of Wight, North & South Downs, Weald, Chilterns and Cotswolds (37 hills).

Figure 1: The division of the books in the 'Hills of England' series.

Volume 2: The Midlands and South Pennines includes the Forest of Dean, Welsh Marches, Shropshire Hills, Clent Hills, Charnwood Forest, Lincolnshire Wolds, Derbyshire Dales & Peak District, Peckforton Hills, South Pennines and Forest of Bowland (42 hills).

Volume 3: Northern England and the Isle of Man includes the Yorkshire Wolds, North York Moors, Yorkshire Dales, North Pennines, Kielder Forest, Simonside Hills, Cheviots, Lakeland and the Isle of Man (54 hills).

The Mountains of England

England's Highest Peaks details all the 2,000ft (610m) summits of England, including Dartmoor, Black Mountains, Peak District, Yorkshire Dales, North Pennines, Cheviots, Lakeland and the Isle of Man. It is written and presented in the same style as *The Hills of England* series (52 mountains).

Note: Potts Moor is included in *The Hills of England*, Vol 3, as well as *England's Highest Peaks*, as there is doubt as to whether its summit is above or below 2,000ft (610m). This explains why the hills would appear to total in all four books to 185 instead of 184.

Some beautiful summits have been excluded from the selection described in this book but, in the vast majority of cases, these are simply the summits of vast rolling sections of downland or otherwise indistinct tops or shoulders. By keeping to the strict criterion of a 492ft (150m) descent outlined above, this book has the advantage that every hill described really is worth climbing. All the summits are pronounced and distinct, both on the ground and in the view from the surrounding valleys and hills. In many cases, the views from their summits are absolutely superb and, although they may seem widely spaced in places, it is rare that another separate summit is not visible, at least on a clear day.

Although the higher summits are seen as a more fulfilling challenge by many ardent hillwalkers, the lower hills should not be dismissed or postponed as they are equally as rewarding in terms of natural beauty. The Scottish Munros, with summits above 3,000ft (914m), get many more visitors than the Corbetts, Scottish summits between 2,500ft (762m) and 3,000ft (914m). However, although the Corbetts are not as high as the Munros, the views they have of their higher neighbours are spectacular and reveal hidden corners and corries that the dogged Munro bagger would not even know existed.

The same is certainly true of the hills in much of northern England (Vol 3), particularly the Lake District. However, here, in southern England, these hills *are* the highest summits. They are the 'Munros' of southern England, commanding views that are just as far-reaching as the views from the summits of Scottish mountains. As such, it seems remarkable that so few people have climbed to all the summits in this book. It is even stranger that fewer hillwalkers still have climbed to the summits of all the separate hills and mountains of England. A total of 2,530 people had registered as having climbed all the 277 Scottish Munros by June 2001 and this total is increasing at the rate of about 150 to 230 each year; 366 people have also climbed all of the 517 Munro Tops. In contrast, the summiteers of the separate English summits are only just creeping into double figures.

There are certainly some summits that are best left to those committed walkers who intend to do them all. Few will find much interest in climbing Hensbarrow Beacon (Section 1), surrounded as it is by spoil-mountains from the china clay works. The museum nearby is far more interesting. Carnmenellis (again in Section 1) lies on private land where there is no agreed access, likewise the summit of Sheepcote Hill in Volume 2. These summits are collector's pieces, not Sunday afternoon strolls. However, it must be said that the summit of Carnmenellis is an outstanding viewpoint.

Perhaps the forthcoming 'right to roam' legislation will help improve access to the summit of the uncultivated moorland of Carnmenellis. In other cases, where this book is concerned, the new legislation will make little difference to the currently agreed voluntary access. The 'right to roam' does not apply to agricultural land, which most of the land crossed in these walks is, even if it is in permanent grassland.

All the summits included in this volume are, without fail, interesting and dominating but there were some unfortunate casualties as a result of applying the 492ft (150m) descent rule. It is a well-known fact in Scotland that the Ordnance Survey can magically declare that a mountain has gained or lost many feet or metres of altitude between editions of maps. However, in England, especially southern England, this is less of a problem and one can be fairly certain that the summit heights and col heights are fairly accurate. However, there are a few summits that fall just short of inclusion and these are listed on page 18.

SUMMIT	HEIGHT	GRID REFERENCE	SECTION	NEAREST 'SEPARATE' SUMMIT
Beacon Hill[1]	142m / 466ft	SS 132448	01	Brown Willy
Mardon Down	356m / 1,168ft	SX 767870	02	High Willhays[2]
Bleadon Hill	176m / 577ft	ST 366571	02	Beacon Batch
Glastonbury Tor	158m / 518ft	ST 512386	02	Beacon Batch
Milk Hill	295m / 968ft	SU 104643	03	Walbury Hill
Bulbarrow Hill	274m / 899ft	ST 777055	03	Lewesdon Hill
Tennyson Down	147m / 482ft	SZ 325853	03	Brighstone Down
Littleton Down	255m / 837ft	SU 941150	04	Butser Hill
Alderton Hill	203m / 666ft	SP 009345	05	Cleeve Hill
Robins Wood Hill	198m / 650ft	SO 840450	05	Cleeve Hill

Notes: 1. Beacon Hill is the highest point on the island of Lundy in the Bristol Channel. 2. High Willhays is the highest summit on Dartmoor and is over 2,000ft (610m) in altitude.

Defining Separateness Precisely

This seemingly pointless definition will take on some significance over the course of this book; it is important to define which landscape features can be used to mark a summit and/or make up the 492ft (150m) descent required to define a hill as separate. For the purposes of this book, summits have been taken as the highest point that looks – or at least appears to be – natural. This includes grassed-over ancient burial mounds but not china clay spoil heaps, for example. The tops of towers, masts and other such paraphernalia are excluded from the process of defining a summit.

In defining the col height between two summits, the height of the lowest point on the ridge that the walker must theoretically cross *on the ground* is used. Thus, railway cuttings are included but bridges over railway cuttings are not. These are not simply pedantic meanderings: Swyre Head (Section 3) is included because its grassed-over summit mound provides the final few feet for the 492ft (150m) rule; Nine Barrow Down (Section 3) is included because the Swanage to Corfe Castle railway cutting lowers the col between it and Swyre Head at Harman's Cross by a few critical feet; the china clay spoil heaps that tower over the summit of Hensbarrow Beacon (Section 1) are *not* included in the measurement of the height of its summit.

For most walkers, however, these details make very little difference because, to be honest, a summit is just as worth climbing whether it is surrounded by a 489ft (149m) descent or one of 492ft (150m)! However, for the purposes of writing this book, an exact definition needs to be developed. Swyre Head, Nine Barrow Down and the 'natural' summit of Hensbarrow Beacon are all included in Dawson's table.

The Routes

Due to the decline in public transport, particularly in rural areas, many walkers will use cars to reach the hills that they wish to climb. As a result, the routes in this book all start and finish at the same point, where car parking space is available. However, in some places, space may be limited and this is mentioned in the text where appropriate.

With this in mind, every walk is circular except in a few cases where this is not possible, specifically Carnmenellis (Section 1) and Hensbarrow Beacon (Section 1). Each route climbs the mountain in the most interesting way, although this may not necessarily be the quickest, shortest or easiest approach.

As most of the hills lie in popular tourist areas, there is usually no shortage of accommodation of any kind. However, this may not be the case in parts of the south-east (Section 4) and North Wessex Downs (Section 3) and in these areas it may be particularly advisable to make arrangements in advance. Also, coastal and upland areas, such as Lyme Regis (Section 3), Cornwall (Section 1) and Exmoor (Section 2), are very busy in the summer and it is becoming increasingly important to pre-book accommodation.

As already mentioned, the walks are mostly circular and, as all routes from a hilltop involve a descent, all the walks involve some degree of climbing. In fact, most routes begin at, or at least reach, the local valley level at some point, if for no other reason than to give a circle of meaningful length and interest. However, the climb to the summit also ties in with the idea of quality being the determining factor. It is generally much more satisfying to have climbed to a given summit from a natural valley level, or the closest practicable point to it, than it is to ascend from a higher level starting point. Of course, if you wish to park close to the summit, as is often possible in the south-east (Section 4) and other areas, then you will probably have to accept that a circular walk is not possible and a short stroll is the only option.

In the most popular areas, there is no shortage of public rights of way. These were originally designed to allow local people to reach church from outlying farms and habitations. As such they were not originally intended for the heavy usage that many of them receive today and, thus, courtesy and respect should be shown at all times for the landowner's land and property. After the hillwalker's code (below) the mutual rights of walkers and landowners are outlined. Not all paths are visible on the ground, however. Across large grass fields, the route may be far from clear if not waymarked and compass bearings are therefore occasionally given in the text. In such cases, it would be advisable to carry a compass and know how to use it. Also, some of the footpaths and routes described may not be public rights of way, especially on open moorland where access is not normally a problem. However, care should be taken not to abuse this trust. It is important to remember that the hills are part of estates and farms and the following code is recommended to minimise conflicts between walkers and landowners or farmers.

A Hillwalker's Code (Based on the Countryside Code)

1. Avoid damage to fences, gates and walls. When fences and walls must be crossed, use stiles and gates where possible.
2. Boundaries have an important function, to keep livestock either in or out. Leave closed gates closed. Conversely, gates may have been left deliberately open to make larger fields, so leave them as you find them. However, in cases where there is a specific instruction to shut the gate, this should be followed regardless.
3. Keep to footpaths and other rights of way where this is possible. Do not damage crops.
4. Respect other people's belongings; leave farm machinery alone.
5. Keep dogs under control. You should always have your dog on a lead and this is particularly important on the open hill or in fields containing livestock. Dogs pose a threat not only to livestock but also

to wild animals. Remember, they live there throughout the year, it is their home – do not disturb them. Also remember that it is within a farmer's legal rights to shoot a dog found worrying his sheep.

6. Do not leave litter. Dispose of organic debris such as tea bags discreetly under stones or better still take them home. Take special care with cigarettes, matches and anything else that could cause a fire. Dry moorland and the underlying peat can burn very easily and quickly get out of control.

7. Keep to the right and in single file when walking on country roads – 'face oncoming traffic'. Also remember that drivers may not be expecting to find walkers on their roads. It is particularly important to employ common sense when walking along roads. Although you should generally keep on the right-hand side, you should cross to the left-hand side before walking around sharp right-hand bends to make yourself visible. Not all drivers drive at a speed at which they can stop quickly, especially in southern England.

8. Do not pick wild flowers – it may be illegal and they can be enjoyed by all if they are left where they are.

9. Tread carefully on eroded paths. Do not create erosion scars by shortcutting hairpin bends or widening wet or muddy footpaths. If a footpath is too wet or boggy to walk on, do not walk on the edge, which will cause erosion, but on vegetated ground a few yards away on either side.

10. Do not build extra cairns in upland areas – too many can be a hindrance rather than a help. However, conversely do not demolish any existing ones; someone else may be relying on them. Cairns on summits, however, are different as they are an indication of the highest point and a measure of achievement.

11. Make no unnecessary noise – it only serves to disturb the scene and other people's enjoyment. As well as disturbing local wildlife, the owners of isolated country houses may be trying to enjoy a peaceful afternoon in their gardens.

12. Try to keep streams and rivers clean. They are often used as the basis for the drinking water supply to isolated villages and farms.

Adhere to this code – other people's livelihood, enjoyment and welfare depend on your doing so.

Potential dangers

1. Attacks by cattle upon humans are becoming increasingly common. Whilst it is illegal to keep a dairy bull in a field with a public right of way running through it, it is perfectly legal to keep a beef bull with a herd of cows in a field to which the public have access. When they are with cows, bulls are normally not interested in passers-by, but it is still wise to check for a bull, avoid it and keep an eye on it at all times. Young bullocks and heifers may express an interest in walkers but usually this is nothing more than curiosity. Cows with calves pose a more serious problem. A cow will attack any person or animal (particularly dogs) that she sees as a potential threat to either her or her calf. The vast majority of recent attacks, most of which have led to either serious injury or in some cases death, are due to dog owners being attacked as they try to help their dog.

   Cattle are frequently to be found in the pastures of southern England. If you must walk your dog through a field with cattle then keep your dog on a lead and as far away from the herd as is possible. Keep an eye on the cattle and keep close to a boundary that you can cross if necessary. If your dog is attacked by cattle then leave the dog and get away as quickly as possible – dogs are smaller and more agile and certainly much less likely to come to harm than you are. The important thing to remember is that well-behaved dogs on leads can provoke cattle, as well as those that are unleashed.

2. With the exception of wilder areas, such as Bodmin Moor (Section 1), the hills of southern England do not support the dangerous 'bottomless' peat bogs that are to be found further north. However, do not be too complacent. Wet clay soils can also be very dangerous as the ground can be extremely greasy and slippery.

   Clay is also churned up by farm animals, particularly cattle, forming tricky quagmires. Although these are not bottomless, they can be dangerous. In the Weald of south-east England (Section 4), the Gault and Wealden clays are particularly notorious. The Gault Clay delayed and disrupted the construction of the M20 around Maidstone, even with modern equipment. Clay is notoriously sticky and, on one occasion, a member of a local walking group got stuck in the Gault Clay of the Weald. In the end, one boot simply had to be left in the clay – it could not be removed – whilst the trapped member was carried to safety.

   Although this may be an extreme case, most soils contain a certain amount of clay and, in wetter periods, many soil types can cause a problem. Bearing stories like the above in mind, it is better to be cautious when crossing large quagmires. Accept that somebody may get stuck and, if you are part of a group, try to stagger your crossing in case you all get stuck at once!

Public Rights of Way: Your Rights and Those of the Landowner

The landowner or occupier's rights and responsibilities
1. A farmer may shoot a dog found worrying his sheep. However, as dogs should be on a lead, as mentioned below, this conflict should not arise.
2. A farmer may not plough or otherwise disturb a right of way running around the *edge* of a field.
3. A farmer may plough or disturb a footpath or bridleway crossing the field (i.e. not running around the edge) for agricultural purposes, although its surface *must*, by law, be restored within two weeks.
4. The farmer or occupier must not block the right of way by erecting a fence, wall or hedge without providing some reasonable means of crossing it. Take care with electric fences, on which crossing points are often provided by means of detaching the wire by unclipping it using an insulated grip. If no such crossing point is provided then the fence is an illegal obstruction. However, as they are normally low, they can be crossed by pulling the top strand of wire down using some sort of insulating material, e.g. jumper, handkerchief etc. They are generally a very low current but they may nevertheless give you a very nasty shock. This affects some people more than others.

Your rights and responsibilities
1. You can use a public right of way, provided you are legally entitled, as detailed below. You can do so without intimidation.
2. You can stop by the right of way, although you should *never* block it.
3. Provided your dog is under control and *on a lead*, you are legally allowed to take it with you.
4. At the edge of the field, you are allowed to walk the following widths: footpaths: 4½ ft (1½ m), bridleways: 10ft (3m), byways: 16ft (5m).
5. Across fields, you are allowed to walk the following widths: footpaths:

3ft (1m), bridleways: 6½ft (2m), byways: 10ft (3m). Any person or notice advising you otherwise is illegal.

6. If a crop has been planted across a right of way, you are still allowed to walk its route, provided that you only damage any crops within the widths above. Outside these, you are liable to be prosecuted for criminal damage. No person may intimidate you from walking along a right of way; farmyard dogs do not qualify in this respect, provided they are not causing an 'obstruction'. If, however, they attack you, you have a claim against the landowner or occupier.

7. If the path is obstructed then you are entitled to travel the shortest and least-damaging route around it. This includes both natural and artificial obstructions.

8. You must follow all legal footpath diversions, as authorised by the highways department of the local council.

Rights of Way definitions

A *footpath* is a right of way that only walkers are allowed to use. Walkers, cyclists and horseriders may use a *bridleway*. All traffic, including off-road vehicles, may use a *byway*. It should, however, be noted that farmers or occupiers may, of course, use the tracks as they wish. Thus, for example, although a footpath should in theory by reserved for foot traffic, the farmer may, and is entitled to, use it as a farm road.

At least in theory these rights and rules work well to the advantage of both parties. Unfortunately, there are those on both sides who fail to respect them. This is no reason to avoid following the right of way, although you should show care and extra consideration towards the farmer or occupier if they have shown to be unwilling to provide access, perhaps by ploughing up paths etc. However, before entering into a dispute with a farmer or occupier, remember that you are not allowed to use physical force to exercise your rights. You may also like to consider that guns are often kept on isolated farms. An unfriendly farmer or occupier may, in their blinkered vision, see you as a trespasser. This, however, is an extreme scenario and, apart from the ploughing of fields and removing signs, few further problems are likely to arise.

At-a-glance Grids and the Grading System

A grid accompanies each route, showing the difficulty of terrain, difficulty of navigation and quality. The name, metric and imperial heights, OS grid reference, OS Landranger Sheet number, distance, time and starting point are also shown.

The timings are calculated by assuming that for every 1,000ft (305m) of ascent undertaken, an average walker could cover 2 miles (3km) on the level. An average walking pace over the whole route of 1½ miles per hour is then used to work out the given time. Obviously, this speed will differ from walker to walker and a small difference is given on either side of the calculated time to allow for this. However, on the short routes, which are designed to be completed in an afternoon, the time allowed for lunch is minimal, whereas, on the routes of middle length, if you plan to complete them on a long summer's afternoon, you may wish to take off twenty minutes to half an hour to compensate for the lunch break, which, presumably, would not be taken. However, if you make a long stop for a cream tea, drink at a pub or a pub lunch on the walk then you will probably have to add on this time.

The gradings below are used throughout the series and are similar to those used in *England's Highest Peaks*. In southern England, there are not really any routes that can be classified as scrambles of any severity. Having said that, however, the rocks of Rough Tor on the Brown Willy route (Section 1) do provide options for scrambling.

(i) **Terrain gradings**

All the routes in the series are walks or simple scrambles so there is therefore little difference in technical difficulty. However, terrain does differ considerably and the grading is based upon the table below. It is fair to comment that Grade 1 routes are suitable for all the family in good weather and/or underfoot conditions, Grades 2 and 3 are more serious walking and Grades 4 and 5 are simple scrambles.

1. Easy terrain
2. Steep and/or arduous over short distances
3. Appreciable sections of rough, difficult ground
4. Some handwork may be required in places
5. Longer unavoidable sections of simple scrambling

(ii) **Navigation gradings**

It is assumed that, other than for odd occasions where a compass bearing is given in the text, there will be no problem with navigation in clear weather. The gradings listed below are the worst possible, i.e. in misty conditions, which do occur on the hills of southern England. Under a covering of snow, Grades 1 to 3 become 4 and Grade 4 becomes 5.

1. Clear paths; easy to follow in mist
2. A few pathless sections but a compass is unlikely to be required
3. Some pathless sections on which a compass may be needed
4. Long pathless sections over which a map and compass are necessary
5. Featureless – a high standard of navigation required in bad weather

(iii) **Quality gradings**

Quality is very subjective so there will be many different opinions. With these gradings, I have tried to keep my personal interests and experiences out of my mind when assessing each route.

1. Generally dull and uninteresting
2. Some interesting parts
3. Interesting
4. Fine views and good scenery or consistently interesting
5. Excellent – a wide variety of scenery and views

However, as the quality gradings are based on a wide range of factors, some readers may wish to see the hills indexed by subjects of interest and this is shown below.

(Numbers in brackets are section numbers)

Archaeology: Staple Hill (2), Walbury Hill (3), Brighstone Down (3), Swyre Head (3), Chanctonbury Hill (4), Firle Beacon (4), Cleeve Hill (5), Bredon Hill (5).
Caves and potholes: Beacon Batch (2).
Cliffs: Watch Croft (1), Beacon Batch (2), Hardown Hill (3), Swyre Head (3), Nine Barrow Down (3), Cliffe Hill (4), Cleeve Hill (5).
Coastlines: Watch Croft (1), Dunkery Beacon route (2), St Boniface Down (3), Brighstone Down (3), Swyre Head (3), Hardown Hill (3), Nine Barrow Down (3).
Geological interest: Hensbarrow Beacon (1), Brown Willy (1), Dunkery Beacon route (2), Beacon Batch (2), Swyre Head (3), Nine Barrow Down (3), Brighstone Down (3), Leith Hill (4), Botley Hill (4), Crowborough (4), Wilmington Hill (4), Cleeve Hill (5).

Gorges: Beacon Batch (2).
Impressive scenery: All routes awarded a grade four or five for quality.
Moorlands and Heaths: Brown Willy (1), Watch Croft (1), Dunkery Beacon route (2), Wills Neck (2), Beacon Batch (2), Hardown Hill (3), Nine Barrow Down (3), Crowborough (4).
Mining and quarrying: Kit Hill (1), Hensbarrow Beacon (1).
Scrambling: Brown Willy (1).

A question I am frequently asked is what would I consider to be the finest hill of those in southern England. I find this a very difficult question to answer as the quality of any hill depends upon the route taken. However, I have listed below, in order, the summits that I consider to be the ten finest in the book:

1.	Dunkery Beacon (2)	(Exmoor)
2.	Brighstone Down (3)	(Isle of Wight)
3.	Beacon Batch (2)	(Mendips)
4.	Swyre Head (3)	(Purbeck)
5.	Wilmington Hill (4)	(South Downs)
6.	Leith Hill (4)	(Greensand Ridge)
7.	Wills Neck (2)	(Quantocks)
8.	Selworthy Beacon (2)	(Exmoor)
9.	Lewesdon Hill (3)	(Wessex Downs)
10.	Win Green (3)	(Wessex Downs)

Directions

Points of the compass and compass bearings are often given to indicate direction. Compass bearings begin at north (0°) and run through east (90°), south (180°) and west (270°). Any directions such as left and right refer to the direction of travel and walkers following the routes in reverse may have considerable difficulty in following the description. In reference to the banks of rivers and streams, the phrases 'true left' and 'true right' are not used and 'left bank' refers to the left-hand bank and 'right bank' the right-hand bank, both in the direction of travel and not necessarily in the direction in which the water is flowing.

How to Use This Book

Each area is given an introduction in which accommodation and geology are discussed. A map of the region showing the hills, towns and important roads is included to give an understanding of the geography of the region. Each route is given a description and a map to give the reader an idea of the route whilst reading the text.

Those not experienced in walking in southern England may like to read the pages on **General Advice** that follow and those readers with little or no geological knowledge may find the geological descriptions of each section a little more meaningful after reading the **Geological Introduction**. Any terms that may be unfamiliar are explained in the **Glossary** at the back of the book. The **Useful Telephone Numbers** section lists the telephone numbers of all places mentioned in the text and Tourist Information/ National Park Centres. Also, there is a **Reader's Personal Log** for your own records and a section on **Hill Names and their Meanings** for those interested in their derivations.

The words *path* and *track* have been used in the text with very specific meanings that are intended to help readers identify the correct route on the ground. I have defined them as follows:

Path – A strip of ground eroded by the passage of feet, along which it is too narrow to drive an all-terrain vehicle.
Track – A strip of ground eroded by either feet or vehicles so that it is wide enough to drive an all-terrain vehicle along (although this may not be practically possible due to rocks or other obstructions).

Walking Routes in Reverse

There are very few routes that can be reversed without some loss of quality. The routes are planned so as to keep the most impressive views of the scenery ahead rather than behind. Also, use is made of simple, less steep descents at the end of long days. Indeed, many of the descriptions will be difficult, if not impossible, to use in reverse, as what may appear very obvious in one direction may be far from obvious in the other, particularly when walking unwaymarked paths across a complex maze of fields. Therefore, the walking of routes in reverse is not recommended.

The Descriptions

Too often, in my opinion, guidebooks tell you little more than that which can be seen from a 1:25,000 scale map. 'Follow the south ridge from the car park to the summit' is not an adequate description unless the route is very obvious indeed. I have tried to give clear and detailed descriptions to help those using the book. Some authors claim that if the descriptions are too detailed some walkers will feel that they have lost the sense of adventure but, personally, I see the purpose of a guidebook as being to guide. In general, in southern England, a map is not necessary for navigational purposes – this book should be sufficient. However, on the higher summits, specifically, Brown Willy, Watch Croft, the Dunkery Beacon route and on Wills Neck, it would be a good idea to take a 1:50,000 scale map, as these areas have weather conditions of a more mountainous nature: thick mists and low cloud can arise quickly and make navigation difficult. However, you may like to take a map in any case to help identify features in the view that are not specifically mentioned in the text.

The Maps

The route maps are drawn approximately to a 1:50,000 scale (2cm = 1km; 1½ inches = 1 mile) and show only important information to avoid clutter. They are provided to give an idea of the route, not specifically for navigation on the ground in bad weather, as they are not as accurate as an Ordnance Survey map. The section maps are drawn approximately to a 1:625,000 scale (4cm = 25km; 1 inch = 10 miles). Again, unimportant information is excluded to avoid clutter. **All the maps have north at the top. A list of symbols is provided overleaf.** There are some minor variations in the scale of the maps so that they can conveniently be fitted onto a page. However, these variations are small and unlikely to cause any problems.

Key to Route Maps

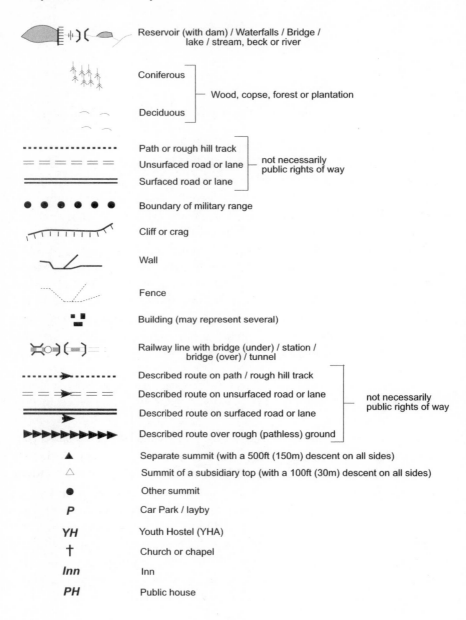

Reservoir (with dam) / Waterfalls / Bridge / lake / stream, beck or river

Coniferous ⎤
⎟ Wood, copse, forest or plantation
Deciduous ⎦

Path or rough hill track ⎤
Unsurfaced road or lane ⎬ not necessarily public rights of way
Surfaced road or lane ⎦

Boundary of military range

Cliff or crag

Wall

Fence

Building (may represent several)

Railway line with bridge (under) / station / bridge (over) / tunnel

Described route on path / rough hill track ⎤
Described route on unsurfaced road or lane ⎟
⎬ not necessarily public rights of way
Described route on surfaced road or lane ⎟
Described route over rough (pathless) ground ⎦

▲ Separate summit (with a 500ft (150m) descent on all sides)

△ Summit of a subsidiary top (with a 100ft (30m) descent on all sides)

● Other summit

P Car Park / layby

YH Youth Hostel (YHA)

† Church or chapel

Inn Inn

PH Public house

Key to Section Maps

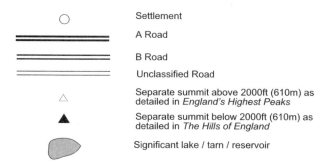

○   Settlement

A Road

B Road

Unclassified Road

△   Separate summit above 2000ft (610m) as detailed in *England's Highest Peaks*

▲   Separate summit below 2000ft (610m) as detailed in *The Hills of England*

Significant lake / tarn / reservoir

Accompanying Maps

As I have already mentioned, on the high uplands of the south-west, this book alone is not satisfactory; a map, compass and knowledge of how to use them are essential. An Ordnance Survey 1:50,000 scale Landranger map of the areas involved will suffice but alternatively all the hills are covered by the Ordnance Survey's Explorer Series at a 1:25,000 scale. Therefore, the following Landranger sheets will be required: 181, 182, 200, 201 and 203 or Explorer sheets: 102, 109 and 140, together with Outdoor Leisure sheet 9.

The rest of the hills are covered by the following Landranger sheets: 150, 163, 165, 174, 183, 184, 186, 187, 188, 189, 192, 193, 195, 196, 197, 198 and 199.

Again, they could be replaced by the following Explorer sheets: 104, 106, 108, 114, 116, 118, 120, 121, 122, 123, 128, 133, 135, 138, 141, 142, 143, 146, 148, 154, 158, 179, 181 and 190, together with Outdoor Leisure sheets 9, 15, 29 and 45.

General Advice

Despite southern England's pleasant climate and relatively tame landscapes, there are certain specific conditions that are not present in the other hill and mountain areas of Britain. Underfoot terrain is not necessarily good and the weather can be testing at times. What is written here is the product of my experience and I would urge walkers who are not perhaps familiar with this part of the country to read what follows.

Weather Conditions

With the highest summit in this book, Dunkery Beacon on Exmoor, reaching an altitude of 1,704ft (519m), it is clear that not all the hills of southern England are in lowland settings. As a result, there are a wide variety of altitudes and associated weather conditions.

The south-west has a reputation for warm weather and short winters but this description relates more to the south coasts of Devon and Cornwall where palm trees flourish outside all the year round in resorts like Falmouth and Torquay. Here, they are sheltered from the prevailing westerly winds that buffet the colder northern coast. In autumn, the region often experiences the warmest temperatures in the whole country but this is also a particularly wet time. Successive Atlantic depressions sweep into the south-west and deposit much of their rain there, rather than further to the east.

Together with this rain, the depressions bring thick swirling mists and fogs that lie over the bleak moorlands of Exmoor, Bodmin Moor and Dartmoor making navigation especially difficult. Nothing should be taken for granted: these rough uplands have a climate more similar to that of the Lake District than the rest of southern England. By this, I mean that whilst they share much of the south's fine weather, this can quickly deteriorate into low cloud as a depression moves in. In these areas, an accurate weather forecast should be sought before departure, although these uplands can generate and attract showers even when a dry day is forecast.

Across south-east England, the weather is generally settled and, in summer, very hot. With the recent trend for summers with temperatures exceeding 25 degrees Celsius on many days, the heat can pose its own problems and it is very easy to get dehydrated or develop a more serious condition, such as heatstroke. Hill fogs also occur across the south-east, although these are generally associated with settled cold conditions and high-pressure systems during the autumn and winter.

When the east wind is blowing, the hills of the south-east are the first thing that the wind strikes after the frozen areas of Russia where it was generated. During this type of weather, the south of England can be as cold as any other part of the country and can easily be the coldest when the wind chill factor is taken into account; days with sub-zero temperatures occur every winter in this 'tame' landscape. On these days, fleeces, gloves and warm hats are imperative. It is also the case that every winter the hills receive some snow meaning that paths are obliterated, although, at least across fields, navigation should not be a problem.

Lightning is much more dangerous on hills than elsewhere. It usually strikes the highest point around and if you are standing on a hilltop, that's you! Keep your feet close together and do not lie down, only crouch. The greater the distance between your extremities, the higher the potential voltage and danger. When the lightning strikes the ground, as the earth has a large resistance, a huge voltage – hundreds of thousands of volts – is created across as little as a couple of feet. This is the cause of most lightning-related deaths rather than direct hits. Get rid of metal equipment (including frame rucksacks) and crouch on your frameless rucksack to help insulate you. Seek low ground and depressions (not those containing water). Do not stand under lone trees or on or near summits, rocky peaks or pinnacles. Move immediately if you hear any kind of static crackling or feel your hair stand on end. Keep a check on thunderstorms. Time the difference in seconds between the lightning flash and hearing the thunder. The bigger the gap then the further away the strike is; if there is no difference then the storm is overhead (very dangerous).

Underfoot Conditions

As mentioned in the introduction, clay soils can be quite awkward and dangerous after wet weather. In addition, when walking in areas such as the Weald (Section 4), the adhesive clay slows progress by sticking thickly to boots and other footwear at all times of the year, except at the peak of summer. Rain also makes steep chalk slopes dangerous, as a thin layer of treacherous silt develops on the surface of paths. In general, there are few places in southern England where paths will not be very muddy and awkward after rain.

The exception to this is on free-draining soils, such as those of the Mendips (Section 2) and the Cotswolds (Section 5), although, again, paths can become slimy and quite muddy. On the uplands of the south-west, the peat moorlands are very wet in winter and only dry out during the summer.

Boots

For most of the year, a good pair of boots is a precondition to successful walking in the south. The wet soils make shoes and trainers impractical, especially as they are not waterproof. Wellington boots are an alternative, although they do not have a very good grip, which can be a problem on slimy paths. A pair of flexible, broken-in, well-fitting leather boots is the best all-round option. For walking in southern England, you only need a pair of 'summer' boots, although if you are planning on walking in winter on hills further to the north then 'four season' boots would be better. Buy a pair that feel comfortable and bear in mind that fabric boots are rarely as waterproof or sturdy as leather ones. Make sure your boots are well dubbed and, if you are on holiday, it is probably a good idea to carry a spare tin of dubbin but, most importantly of all, make sure your boots fit and are broken in! All too often a pair of badly fitted boots can ruin a walking holiday when they cause blisters. However, that said, carrying plasters and a blister kit is always a good idea since, however well your boots may fit, there is always a first time.

Rucksacks

Almost as important as boots is a rucksack, which is an essential walker's tool. It keeps equipment dry and provides a safe and comfortable way of carrying it. I would not recommend frame rucksacks, as they are big, heavy and bulky and become easily wedged in tight, difficult situations. A mesh next to the back is a good idea, as this allows air to circulate and helps stop the back from becoming too hot and sweaty – a particular problem in southern England. Chest and waist straps are also important to look out for. Although most rucksacks now have waist straps, they do not all have chest straps, which are very helpful in distributing weight and load. Outside pockets are another consideration. A good selection of easily accessible pockets and hoops is very important, as it is very awkward to store small things that are in frequent use in the main compartment where they fall to the bottom and become lost amongst larger, bulkier items.

Perhaps the best piece of advice is to buy what feels comfortable in the shop. If possible put some weight in it and walk around. If it is not comfortable in the shop, it certainly will not improve at 1,000ft. As for size, many walkers find 25 litres more than adequate for day expeditions. However, in winter, I usually take a 35-litre rucksack as I find it difficult to fit large bulky jackets and waterproofs into the smaller sizes along with my other equipment.

Whatever it may say on the label, very few rucksacks are actually waterproof and, although sandwich bags will suffice for the outside pockets, a rucksack liner is a good investment for the main compartment since it saves wrapping items up individually.

Clothing

Clothing is certainly very much dependent on the time of year. In the bitter cold of winter, mountain clothing is most appropriate, even this far south, and this consists of three layers – (i) next to skin layer, (ii) insulating layer and (iii) outer shell; these are detailed below. In summer, a T-shirt is also probably more than enough on a hot day. However, you would be well advised to consider buying a 100 per cent polyester garment as detailed for the 'next to skin layer'.

(i) **Next to skin layer**

This is very important and possibly the most critical of the three layers. Except in *very cold* weather, walkers will sweat quite a lot. The layer next to the skin must 'wick' this sweat away from the skin and also off itself and on to another outer layer. If a cotton garment is worn next to the skin, it will become waterlogged and damp leaving your back cold, clammy and sticky. Cotton is sometimes called 'death cloth' because of its notorious reputation of causing hypothermia in the mountains.

The best clothing to wear in this layer consists of 100 per cent polyester. Clothing such as this is quite expensive and, although not always easy to find on the high street, it is available in many outdoor shops. However, as they wick well, they can be dried quickly after washing so you will not need many. A pair of comfortable lightweight trousers are a good idea and, again, it is possible to buy specialist pairs from outdoor shops. Try to avoid trousers with too many buttons, as these are likely to be snagged on rocks and lost.

(ii) **Insulating layer**

The primary function of this layer is to keep you warm. Jumpers, sweatshirts and particularly climbing fleeces may be used. Even though you may feel cold to start with, it is a mistake to put too much on too soon. You will soon get hot when you start walking and will end up hot and sweaty and then unable to take anything off. Instead, add it as you feel you need it. It is always necessary to keep one or two extra layers to put on when stopping for any length of time. In cold conditions, you should also consider carrying gloves, a woolly hat and a scarf.

(iii) **Outer shell**

The function of this layer is to keep you dry – not warm. A breathable fabric, such as Gore Tex, is essential. It must keep the rain and wind from getting in but also let perspiration out. It is only necessary to put this on when the rain starts and must consist of waterproof trousers as well as a jacket with a hood. Remember, just because a weather forecast promises a fine day, this does not guard against heavy showers, which are easily generated on an apparently fine day in the uplands. Finally, a pair of sunglasses may also be a good idea during the summer months.

Heat and Sun

Before setting off walking on a hot summer's day, there are a number of medical conditions of which you should be aware.

(i) **Sunburn**

There is nothing unknown about sunburn but remember that the sun is much stronger in the south than areas further to the north. On a long day out in the open, it is quite possible to get very badly burnt, although the degree of this will depend on your own sensitivity. The UV light that causes sunburn may also cause skin cancer if the skin is exposed for too long. Prevention is the best defence and there are many suncreams and sunblocks on the market. These contain a number of chemicals that absorb ultraviolet frequencies of light and they may also contain reflective materials, such as zinc compounds. Arms and legs that are left uncovered for the first time in the season are particularly vulnerable, as is the back of the neck. In addition, prolonged exposure to sunlight can also cause rashes and other minor complaints with some individuals.

(ii) **Dehydration**

This is often the prelude to heatstroke, which follows quickly after sweating stops. The body loses fluid mainly through sweating and urinating, although diarrhoea is another possible loss. To avoid this condition, you should regularly drink plenty of fluids, preferably water rather than other types of drinks, which I find make me more thirsty. If you stop sweating or your urine is particularly dark then you are becoming dehydrated. However, everybody sweats different amounts so the exact amount you should drink is different for each individual, although the equivalent of a cup every half an hour is the average.

(iii) **Heatstroke**

Heatstroke, also known as sunstroke, is the opposite of hypothermia.

The first symptoms are those of heat exhaustion – tiredness and/or feeling faint. However, in heatstroke, the body temperature rises to dangerous levels, more than those experienced in an average dose of flu. The main symptom is a change in mental state. The victim may become confused or uncooperative and this is often accompanied by a rapid pulse, headache, weakness and flushed skin. Treatment should be administered quickly; take the patient to a shady area and help them to cool down by fanning or splashing on water. Fluids should be given if the patient is able to drink, not only to help reduce the body temperature, but also to help with dehydration, which often accompanies and precedes heatstroke. If untreated, heatstroke can be fatal.

Geological Introduction

The geological descriptions that follow in the introductions to each section are generally intended to be fairly self-explanatory. However, this introduction should help readers with little or no knowledge of science and geology to make more sense of what follows. The glossary contains explanations of many of the geological terms that are used throughout the book.

There are three types of rock: sedimentary, igneous and metamorphic. *Sedimentary rocks* form most English landscapes and they are mainly formed from sediments, such as muds or the skeletons of dead sea creatures, on the sea floor. These are then compacted by further sediment, which is deposited above them and they turn into rock. The carcases of sea creatures are often mixed through the mud rather than forming the rock totally or being crushed beyond recognition. They appear in cliffs and other exposures and are called *fossils*. The knowledge of where and when they lived allows geologists not only to date the rock but also suggest the conditions in which it was deposited. Limestones, shales and mudstones are all usually fossiliferous rocks that are formed on the sea floor.

However, sedimentary rocks do not only originate under the sea; some identical rocks are formed in inland lakes and lagoons. Others are formed on dry land or beaches. Sandstones and gritstones are examples of rocks formed on a beach. The process of compaction is the same as that under the sea but obviously this rock will contain no marine fossils. Other sandstones are formed in deserts. Where plants grow profusely, such as in tropical swamps, their remnants collapse into wet ground and do not decompose normally. Instead, they form peat, which is then compacted into coal, a fossil fuel.

Igneous rocks are lavas which may have erupted from a volcano or been forced under pressure into existing rocks; when this happens it is called an igneous intrusion. All igneous rocks begin as magma in the earth's mantle, which is forced to the surface as a result of movements in the crust, often close to a tectonic plate boundary. The type of rock formed will depend not only on whether it formed above or below ground but also on its chemical composition. All igneous rocks are made up of crystals and contain no fossils. The size of the crystals is dependent upon the speed at which the rocks cooled. If the eruption took place under the sea, the rock will have small crystals as a result of the rapid cooling effect of the seawater but if it intruded into other rocks and cooled underground, the process would have been much slower and larger crystals would have been able to form. Finally, if the lava erupted onto dry land, the rock will have medium-sized to small crystals. However, some igneous rocks with large crystals are now exposed in areas such as Dartmoor. Here, the rocks into which the lava intruded have since been worn away. Granite, gabbro, dolerite and basalt are all examples of igneous rocks.

Where an igneous rock came into contact with a sedimentary rock, the igneous rock would bake the sedimentary rock, causing it to melt before crystallising out. This type of rock is known as *metamorphic*. Metamorphic rocks are also formed when other types of rock are subjected to intense pressure. Marble is the metamorphic version of limestone whilst slates are the metamorphic version of shales.

Most of the sedimentary rocks that are seen today were deposited in very different conditions to those in which they now sit. Coal, for example, was deposited in tropical swamps, limestone in tropical shelf-seas and on coral reefs and some sandstones in desert conditions. The reason for this is that, hundreds of millions of years ago, Britain lay just to the north of the equator. In fact, 270 million years ago, all the continents of the earth formed one huge land mass known as Pangaea. They have since diverged due to the movement of the earth's tectonic plates – subdivisions of the earth's crust which are able to move independently; Britain lies on the Eurasian plate.

At their edges, plates are in contact with their neighbours. However, depending upon the motion of the plates relative to each other there can be four types of margin. At a *constructive* margin, the two plates pull apart and magma rises up from the earth's mantle below to fill the gap. This occurs mainly under the oceans where undersea ridges, such as the Mid-Atlantic Ridge, are being formed. The new segments of the earth's crust created by these eruptions are known as oceanic crust and are much denser than continental crust. At a *destructive* margin, dense oceanic crust pushes against less dense continental crust. Here, the denser oceanic crust sinks below the continental crust in what is called a subduction zone. The oceanic crust then melts, causing a build-up of pressure below the surface which is relieved by earthquakes and volcanic eruptions. This is what is happening in the West Indies, with volcanoes such as the one on Montserrat forming.

The third type of margin is called a *collision* boundary and here continental crust collides with continental crust. The result is the crumpling and contortion of the crust to form faults, thrust-planes, anticlines and synclines, as described below. In general, these features form as part of a range of 'fold mountains' and a period of mountain building is called an *orogeny*. The Himalayas and the Alps are both ranges of fold mountains. Finally, two plates can slide past each other at a *transform* margin. This causes violent earthquakes as the plates move. The San Andreas Fault in California is probably the most famous example of a transform margin.

Sedimentary rocks, and most lavas, form regular horizontal layers when they are deposited. Today, however, there are relatively few areas with horizontal bedding or *strata*. Mountain building crumples the crust and forms gentle dips and rises as well as tight folds and even overfolds. The formation of *anticlines* and *synclines* is shown in figure 2, which also explains how they form certain landscapes today.

When the crust breaks and moves separately, a *fault* forms. Faults can be seen where one block of land has risen or fallen relative to the surrounding crusts. Also, a block of land can slide horizontally relative to the surrounding crust in the same way as a transform margin above. Britain contains many fault lines: for example, the famous Craven Faults in the Yorkshire Dales (Volume 3), the Church Stretton Fault in Shropshire (Volume 2) and the Great Glen Fault in Scotland. Faulting and another major principle of geology, that of *unconformity*, is explained in figure 3.

Since Britain moved to its current northern latitude, successive changes in temperature have caused the melting of ice in hotter periods and the spread of ice in colder periods; these cold periods are called *ice ages*. Britain in many ways leads a charmed life in its present position. Despite lying on the same latitude as the frozen wastes of Siberia and Labrador, Britain experiences a much milder, temperate climate. This is due to a warm ocean current, known as the Mid-Atlantic Drift, which, along with

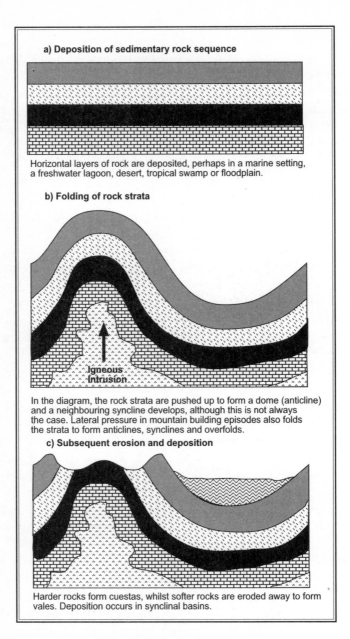

a) Deposition of sedimentary rock sequence

Horizontal layers of rock are deposited, perhaps in a marine setting, a freshwater lagoon, desert, tropical swamp or floodplain.

b) Folding of rock strata

Igneous Intrusion

In the diagram, the rock strata are pushed up to form a dome (anticline) and a neighbouring syncline develops, although this is not always the case. Lateral pressure in mountain building episodes also folds the strata to form anticlines, synclines and overfolds.

c) Subsequent erosion and deposition

Harder rocks form cuestas, whilst softer rocks are eroded away to form vales. Deposition occurs in synclinal basins.

Figure 2: Formation of anticlines and synclines.

a) Deposition of sedimentary rock sequence

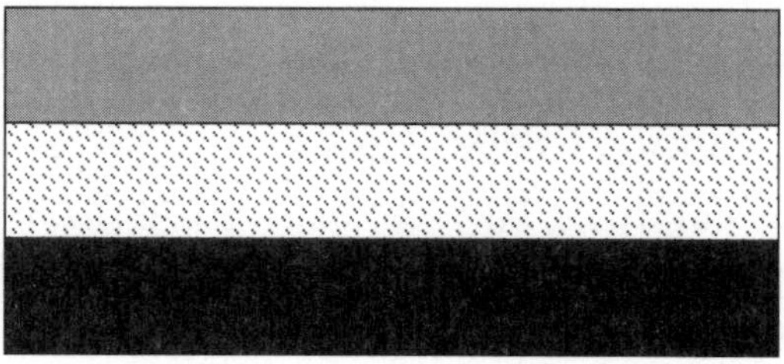

Horizontal layers of rock are deposited, perhaps in a marine setting, a freshwater lagoon, desert, tropical swamp or floodplain.

b) Subsequent transformation of rock strata and landscape

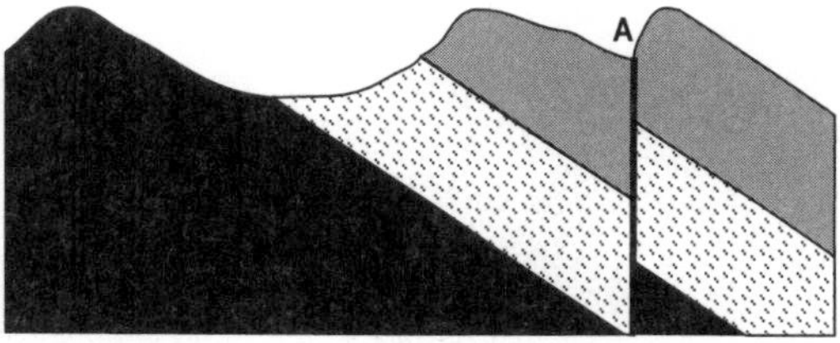

A

Deposition halts, perhaps because of a fall in sea level etc., and the rock strata can be deformed in various ways. Here, a mountain building episode has uplifted the land and set the strata at an angle. At the same time, the fault at A formed as the block of land on the left dropped relative to that on the right. Erosion formed a complex land surface, in which softer rocks form vales and more resistant rocks form hills and ridges.

c) Development of an unconformity

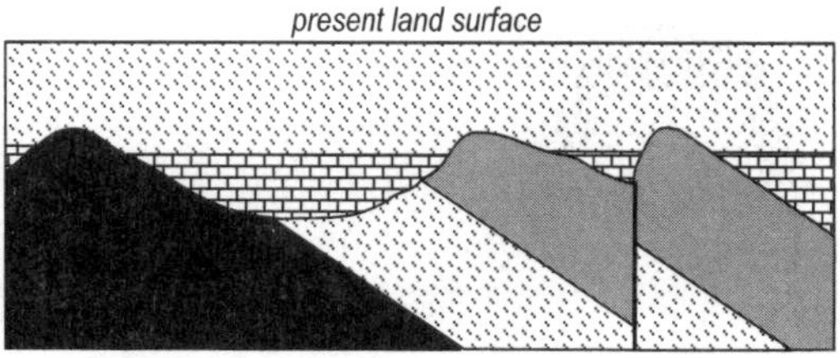

present land surface

After a halt in deposition, sediments again begin to form. Perhaps, for example, the sea has covered the land. Horizontal layers of new rock now begin to form on top of the eroded landscape from (b). This interruption in deposition and strata is called an *unconformity*, which shows that there has not been continuous deposition since (a).

Figure 3: Formation of a landscape over many millions of years.

the Gulf Stream, brings tropical water northwards from the Bay of Mexico. It is in fact a convection current: warm, less-dense water on the surface is drawn northwards from the Bay of Mexico to replace cooler, denser water which has sunk further to the north around the west coast of Britain and Ireland. This cold water is then, at depth, drawn back in the opposite direction to replace the warm water that moves northwards from the Gulf of Mexico. This process is the same as what happens to the air in a room when a radiator or fan heater is turned on.

However, for this process to work, the water must be salty. If a large amount of fresh water enters the North Atlantic, for example from the bursting of a massive continental lake or much higher rainfall, the convection current ceases and the seas around north-western Europe suddenly become much colder. Contrary to historical opinion, this change does not necessarily happen over hundreds of years but could take place in as little as 20 years if the conditions are right.

As Britain is quite a small island, its climate is very dependent on the oceans surrounding it. As a larger amount of energy is required to heat water than soil, water retains its heat in winter and remains cool in summer (water has a higher specific heat capacity). This is why Britain can never experience the extremes of temperature that can be felt in places at the centre of large continents, such as Moscow, which have freezing winters and very hot summers. Therefore, when the sea is warmed by the Mid-Atlantic Drift, Britain's climate is not only stable but warm as well. However, when the sea is not warmed, Britain's climate suddenly changes to one that is still stable but very cold.

The 'freak' events that release the amount of fresh water necessary to interrupt the Mid-Atlantic Drift occur very infrequently from a human perspective but in terms of geological timescale, they have taken place several times and caused rapid changes in temperatures – as much as ten degrees Celsius in a hundred years. It is likely that such events, in connection with variations in the earth's orbit, caused cold periods and ice ages, separated by warmer interglacial periods, such as we are in today. The last ice age was known as the Dimlington Stadial, which lasted for about 10,000 years. Together with a minor readvancement of the ice, known as the Loch Lomond Stadial, this period is referred to as the Ice Age. During the Middle Ages, between AD 1450 and AD 1850, there was a cooling of the British climate known as the Little Ice Age. It peaked around 1680 when 'Frost Fairs' were held in London on the frozen Thames. This was caused by a reduction in the amount of water convected in the Mid-Atlantic Drift due to the presence of a largish amount of fresh water in the North Atlantic, which, although not large enough to stop the convection current altogether, did weaken it sufficiently to cool Britain's climate severely. In no ice age did the glaciers come far enough south to erode the landscape of southern England directly but during the last ice age, Britain became separated from the continent and the Goring Gap was formed (see Section 4).

It is rather ironic that, due to the effects of global warming, Britain may enter another cold period in the very near future. One of the effects of global warming will be an increase in rainfall over the North Atlantic. This, coupled with the melting of the Arctic ice sheets, would introduce a huge amount of fresh water into the North Atlantic. Scientists disagree as to whether this will actually reach the critical quantity necessary to interrupt the Mid-Atlantic Drift but it is generally agreed that it will come very close.

The Geological Timescale

When geologists talk about time, what they are referring to is time in relation to a geological scale, spanning 3,750 million years of the earth's history. Therefore, what they may consider to be a short period of time may be 10,000 years and quite easily more.

Names are given to separate periods in the earth's history, some of which have easily recognisable meanings, for example Carboniferous means coal-forming (coal is a form of carbon), and Devonian refers to the time when the main rock system of Devon was deposited. Figure 4 shows the geological timescale as well as giving an overview of the formation of the hill landscapes of southern England.

Era	Period		Age (millions of years ago)	Overview of the formation of the hills of southern England
Tertiary (Alpine orogeny)	Quaternary	Holocene	0	An arctic tundra covers southern England during the ice ages. English Channel formed by impounded glacial meltwater.
		Pleistocene	2	
	Neocene	Pliocene	7	
		Miocene	24	
	Palaeogene	Oligocene	38	Atlantic Ocean starts to form causing Britain to rise to the north and west.
		Eocene	54	
		Palaeocene	65	Alpine folding forms the Wealden anticline and its neighbouring synclines and fold structures. Fresh water and marine deposits form in these synclinal basins.
Mesozoic	Cretaceous		146	Wealden Beds deposited on a huge floodplain in south-east England, followed by marine sandstones, clays and chalk across the whole country.

	Jurassic	208	Oolitic limestones of the Cotswolds deposited in a shallow sea.
Mesozoic	Triassic	245	New Red Sandstones deposited in desert conditions.
(Amorican orogeny)	Permian	290	Granite intrusion under south-west England forms Mendip anticline.
Palaeozoic	Carboniferous	363	Culm Measures deposited in deep water over Cornwall and West Devon. Mountain Limestone deposited in the Mendips in a shallow sea.
	Devonian	409	A largely marine sequence of rocks is deposited in Cornwall, Devon and Somerset.
(Caledonian orogeny)	Silurian	439	
	Ordovician	510	
	Cambrian	544	
	Precambrian	570 to 3800	

Figure 4: The geological timescale and an overview of the formation of the landscape of southern England.

Section 1 – The Cornish Hills

The Cornish county boundary from the English Channel, along the River Tamar and then overland to the Irish Sea near Welcombe. The Cornish coast from there back to the Tamar estuary.

NAME	HEIGHT	IN SECTION	IN ENGLAND	IN BRITAIN
Brown Willy	420m / 1377ft	01 of 05	101 of 184	1164 of 1552
Kit Hill	334m / 1096ft	02 of 05	120J of 184	1317J of 1552
Hensbarrow Beacon	312m / 1025ft	03 of 05	135 of 184	1360 of 1552
Carnmenellis	252m / 828ft	04 of 05	160J of 184	1456J of 1552
Watch Croft	252m / 828ft	05 of 05	160J of 184	1456J of 1552

Windswept granite moorlands, contorted coastlines and deep, twisting valleys are all reasons why so many tourists come to visit Cornwall. However, its main scenic attraction is that, although it is part of the British highlands, its relief is comparatively subdued and, as such, it provides a contrast to the tamer areas of England while not being as severe as Snowdonia or Scotland. Cornwall's geology was almost exclusively set in the Devonian and Carboniferous periods and its rocks display a marine sequence of sandstones, shales and limestones that have been intruded at depth by a mass of molten granite in the late Carboniferous period.

At the beginning of the Devonian, North America had collided into northern Europe, joining what is now England and Scotland together and creating a chain of fold mountains called the Caledonian Mountains. However, in the prevailing hot climate, these were worn down by flash floods and their sediments spread out over the land to the south, including England. Rivers washed further sediments out to an ocean, the northern shoreline of which fluctuated around Somerset and Bristol, and, south of here, a marine rock sequence developed. The landmass thus formed became known as the Old Red Sandstone continent and these continental deposits today form the Brecon Beacons and Black Mountains just across

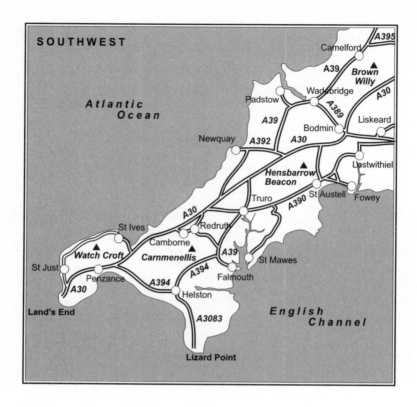

the Welsh border. However, they should not be confused with the New Red Sandstones around Bridgnorth, for example, which are much younger deposits.

The marine sequence of Devon and Cornwall mainly contained less coarse sediments comprising mudstones, which were compacted to shales, thin limestones and sandstones. The alternating layers of rock can be seen along the north Cornish coast where they form a pattern of headlands made up of the toughest rocks, separated by bays where the water has worked to remove the softer sediments. This Devonian rock sequence continues into Devon and Somerset where it forms the uplands of Exmoor and the Quantocks, as well as the coastal scenery around south Dartmoor. These Devonian sediments, which are altogether more complex, are detailed in Section 2.

At the end of the Devonian, the ocean spread northwards and ended up covering much of England, depositing the famous Carboniferous limestones of the Yorkshire Dales and the Mendips, followed by coal from

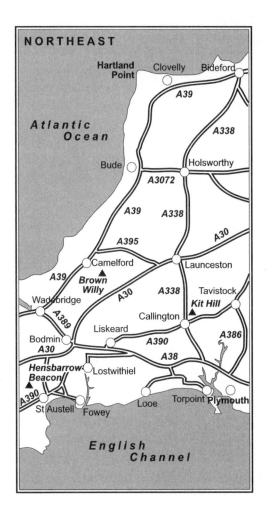

tropical swamps. However, over Devon and Cornwall the ocean was deeper and the Devonian deposition continued in a cyclical sequence of siltstones, mudstones and sandstones. This sequence is called the Culm Measures and formed the final phase of deposition before a massive upheaval that was to transform a deep ocean into an arid desert.

At the end of the Carboniferous, the ocean separating the Old Red Sandstone continent from the only other landmass at the time – Gondwanaland – closed. This formed one huge supercontinent called Pangaea. Located on the southern shore of the Old Red Sandstone continent, southern Britain was subjected to the same folding and faulting that formed the Pyrenees, Appalachians (North America) and the Ural Mountains (Russia). In Devon and Cornwall this had two main effects. Firstly, the lateral pressure formed a large syncline, known as the central Devon syncline, which today exposes all the rocks formed in the Devonian and Carboniferous periods. Moving north-east from Land's End, ignoring the granite moorlands, the Devonian rocks are traversed from oldest to youngest to reach the Carboniferous Culm Measures at the centre of the syncline in the Holsworthy area. Spectacular coastal folds resulting from smaller crumples within the syncline can be seen where the sea has sliced through the deposits. In addition, the pressure caused the mudstones to undergo considerable metamorphosis, transforming them into slates.

The second and more noticeable effect of the Amorican orogeny – as this mountain building epoch is known – was the intrusion of a granite mass under Cornwall and Devon. This occurred later in the orogeny, probably in the early Permian, and formed the Cornish moorlands. At the start of the Amorican movements, volcanic material erupted from undersea vents onto the coastal platform and the subsequent considerable lateral pressure of the main orogeny thrust this material onto the south Cornish coast where it appears on the Lizard Peninsula as well as at Start Point in Devon. The main rock on the Lizard is serpentine – a rare soft dark-green rock, the chemical composition of which is hydrated magnesium silicate – which can be fashioned into decorative rock ornaments.

As the granite intrusion cooled, it developed a network of joints and cracks through which solutions flowed. In the later stages of cooling, hot saline solutions, originating from a lower part of the granite that was still cooling, were forced, under pressure, through these joints and into cracks in the Devonian rocks. In these cracks, the pressure reduced and consequently the solution cooled, allowing many minerals contained in it to be deposited in veins. These minerals included, most notably, cassiterite (tin oxide), wolframite (a tungsten ore), quartz (silica) and feldspars (aluminosilicates of potassium, sodium and calcium). The granites around Land's End and Redruth tend to be richest in tin ores, whereas those around St Austell are richer in feldspars.

Due to the intense pressure of the orogeny, the Devonian rocks were highly deformed, meaning they possessed many cracks or tension faults into which the minerals could be deposited; the richest zones became the principal mining areas. These veins vary in size and length but are generally quite narrow (a few inches to a few feet), quite deep (hundreds of feet) and great distances in length (anywhere between a few hundred yards and a few miles).

The mines, mainly for tin extraction, began as small, opencast affairs, where gangs of men were leased a length of vein by the landowner, which they would then quarry on the surface. Later, however, shaft mining developed as larger companies began operations. It was customary to sink a shaft on or close to the vein and then take off levels to the side at 20m (65ft) intervals. The mining took place on the roofs of these levels, the floor being gradually raised by wooden planking, which has now rotted and is treacherous. Adits that appear on the surface are either horizontal entrances to shafts or drainage channels to remove water from the sump or pool that existed at the bottom of the mine.

The tin that was extracted from the mine was in the form of cassiterite (tin oxide) but mixed with other minerals and rock. A profitable vein would contain over 5 per cent cassiterite, a rich one over 10 per cent and some outstanding ones contained up to 25 per cent. The ore then had to be dressed before it could be smelted. The material would first be washed in a nearby stream to carry away the lighter material and then what was left was finally sorted by hand before the pieces of cassiterite were broken up into a uniform size. They were finally crushed, originally using a heavy iron plate known as a bucker. Later, at the larger smelt mills, iron hammers and rollers were introduced, powered by water-wheels. The crushed ore was then allowed to settle out in water where, being heavier, it sank first before the other lighter waste material.

The final stage in the process is the smelting of the ore. This took place in a furnace, of which the chimneys are widely seen today, and involved adding some form of carbon – coke or charcoal – to reduce (de-oxidise) the cassiterite:

$$\text{\textbf{cassiterite}} + \text{carbon} \rightarrow \text{\textbf{tin}} + \text{carbon monoxide}$$

Overall, it could be expected to obtain at best around 79 tonnes of tin from each 100 tonnes of cassiterite that went into the furnace. However, in total, bearing in mind the relatively low grade of the ore, it was necessary to mine around 17 tonnes of rock for every tonne of tin that left the smelt mill, although this amount was obviously dependent upon the richness of the individual vein. This wastage explains the large amounts of spoil seen today in the landscape around old tin mines. Tin is the basis of a number of important alloys, including bronze (12 per cent tin, 88 per cent copper) and pewter (75 per cent tin, 25 per cent lead).

Cornwall is renowned for its tin industry and relics of this industrial past can be seen across the county from those on Kit Hill to the chimney at Rosemergy at the start of the Watch Croft route near Land's End. The old Cornish tin mining districts are called the stannaries and the miners even had their own regulatory body – the Stannary Parliament. Today, the word stannary, or some derivative, appears in place names across the county.

Although the tin industry in Cornwall is now dead – the last tin mine closed recently – the extraction of another mineral is prospering. The feldspars were affected by water vapours rising from the cooling granite, causing them to become hydrated. This means that water molecules become part of their crystal structure, although this does not make them wet. This formed another mineral, kaolinite (an aluminosilicate), which is more commonly known as china clay. China clay is mined extensively around St Austell, where the giant white spoil heaps of quartz and anhydrous (non-hydrated) feldspars form a 'moonscape' that rises high above the summit of Hensbarrow Beacon. China clay is used in many commodities from toothpaste to the glossy coating for magazine pages, as well as in the manufacture of pottery. Cornwall is one of the largest production areas in the world.

When the molten lava was deposited, it was injected underground where it cooled more slowly than it would have done on the surface and therefore has developed the large crystals and coarse texture of granite. Since it was deposited, the overlying sedimentary deposits have been eroded where the granite lay closer to the surface and today these areas form the moorlands. Here, the granite is generally covered by a thick coating of wet peat, except where it is exposed in tors.

The tors themselves have formed where the surrounding rock has been weathered away. As granite cools, cracks, collectively known as pseudo-joints, appear as a result of both horizontal and vertical shrinkage. In the Tertiary period, rain collected in these cracks and wore away the rock there into sand and gravel. Thus, the tors developed as blocks of more resistant rock with fewer joints. The sand and gravel have since been washed away and the tors left isolated. A process known as exfoliation has also weathered the larger domes. In the desert conditions that existed in the Tertiary and Permian periods, the extreme heat during the day caused the rock to expand while the extreme cold of night caused it to contract. After a while, the outer layers of rock began to flake, giving it an 'onion-skin' appearance. It then disintegrated into granite blocks, known as clitter, which can be seen on the hill slopes today.

The tors were further weathered by the Ice Age. Although the glaciers did not reach this far south, the cold temperatures allowed a large amount of freeze–thaw erosion. As water froze in the smallest cracks, it expanded and, over time, pushed the rock apart. However, others maintain that the biggest single factor in the development of the tors was the warm Tertiary rainfall, which disintegrated the bedrock to a depth of around 20m (65ft).

Thus, the landscape of Cornwall and much of western Devon, Dartmoor in particular, was formed. All the summits in this section lie on granite exposures from Watch Croft on the Land's End peninsula to Kit Hill in the east. Cornwall's highest summit, Brown Willy, forms the highest point of Bodmin Moor, where the 'black beast' is said to roam the wild, bleak and rocky landscape of moor and rough fields. In contrast, the Devonian and Carboniferous rocks form a green and tame landscape around these wild uplands and here, on the tortuous north coast, stand the romantic ruins of Tintagel, the steep cobbled streets of Clovelly and the picturesque fishing village of Padstow alongside the golden sands of the Camel Estuary. In a further contrast, the wooded inlets, curving creeks and tourist resorts of the south Cornish coast form, in general, a much more sheltered scene.

Accommodation

As a popular tourist destination, Cornwall has little shortage of accommodation in any area. In general, the northern coast tends to be rougher, stormier and colder, although towns like Padstow, Newquay and St Ives are popular destinations, with the latter two being popular surfing venues. The south coast is much warmer and the atmosphere is more relaxing, with tourist towns like Penzance, Falmouth and Fowey standing on the edge of large bays or long tidal inlets. It is, however, said that you can always find a good day by going north or south depending on the wind direction. A good base for the whole section would be somewhere central like Bodmin or St Austell. There are youth hostels at Elmscott (near Bude), Boscastle, Tintagel, Treyarnon Bay (between Padstow and Newquay), Perranporth and Land's End on the north coast, with Penzance, Coverack (The Lizard), Boswinger, Golant and Plymouth on the southern coast.

Brown Willy

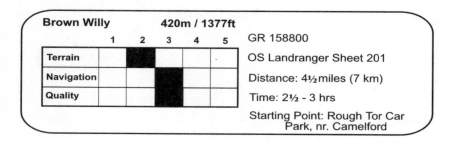

Brown Willy	420m / 1377ft					
	1	2	3	4	5	GR 158800
Terrain		■			·	OS Landranger Sheet 201
Navigation			■			Distance: 4½ miles (7 km)
Quality			■			Time: 2½ - 3 hrs

Starting Point: Rough Tor Car Park, nr. Camelford

Brown Willy is the highest point on and the only separate summit of Bodmin Moor. It is surrounded by a plateau of high ground and rolling hills, which make a low-level starting point difficult. In the past, the ascent has been cited as troublesome because of a lack of access but today a permissive path climbs to the summit, which is less visited than the neighbouring summit of Rough Tor. All around, the wild semi-moorland landscape stretches away devoid of habitations and tracks, making a truly circular route practically impossible but variations can be applied.

The starting point at the Forestry Commission car park at Rough Tor lies at the end of a long dead-end road that leads away eastwards from the A39 on the northern side of the village of Camelford. The car park is a popular place from which to climb up to the rocky granite summit of Rough Tor, the track to which continues from the end of the road down and across a small stream. On the far side, it passes to the left of a fenced enclosure containing a monument to the 43rd Division of the Duke of Cornwall's Light Infantry, which is a replica of the monument on Hill 112 in Normandy. The track then runs more indistinctly over grass towards the rocky upper slopes. Here, a route on grass can be taken to the left or an

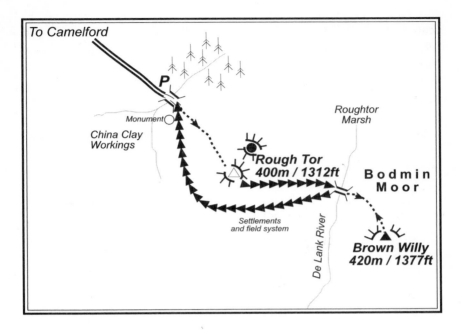

easy scramble leads up through the granite clitter to the summit formations. The highest one is easily surmounted by a simple scramble on its left-hand side and the one to the right, Logan Rock, is most easily climbed by traversing around to its back and going up from there.

Both summits provide a good eastwards view over the De Lank valley below Roughtor Marsh to the slightly higher summit of Brown Willy opposite. The way into the valley is mainly pathless but most people begin by taking off down the valley between the summit tor and Logan Rock. A band of bracken, containing many granite blocks, requires some more delicate steps but below that the grassy common land, which is often grazed by cattle, sheep, ponies and horses, continues down to the valley bottom.

The river is bridged just above the semi-ruined wall on the right where a track begins that climbs the opposite slopes. Over a stile, the climb begins and the route is quite clear as it gradually swings to the right and crosses a further stile before reaching the summit area. The large cairn and trig point then stand atop a mound on the right, from which several more rocky tors stretch away southwards down the ridge.

After reversing the route of ascent back down into the valley, the return can be varied by exploring the ancient settlements and field systems on the left-hand side of Rough Tor. To do so, stay by the wall initially until it swings left and then climbing half left, the route leads up towards the foot of a tongue of bracken. On the way, various rocky banks are crossed. These mark the boundaries in the ancient field system and, in between them, the bracken grows in clear lines running down the slope. These lines of bracken mark the remains of the small ridges and furrows that were used to improve drainage on this poor land.

On reaching the bracken, it soon becomes apparent that it is more extensive than it first appears and that it extends further down the slope than may have been thought. However, a way may be made found through it by means of a network of animal tracks that lead out to the other side. When there, the car park comes into view ahead and a way can be made to it across the intervening grassy pastures. On the way, look out for circular stony banks that are the remains of the ancient settlement that was once here. At first they are difficult to see but look carefully and several will become apparent. Over to the left, modern man's contribution to the landscape – the china clay workings – become increasingly obvious as the return is made past the monument to the car park.

Kit Hill

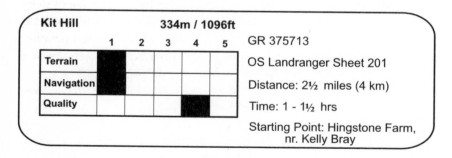

Kit Hill						334m / 1096ft
	1	2	3	4	5	GR 375713
Terrain	■					OS Landranger Sheet 201
Navigation	■					Distance: 2½ miles (4 km)
Quality				■		Time: 1 - 1½ hrs

Starting Point: Hingstone Farm, nr. Kelly Bray

Kit Hill is the most easterly hill in Cornwall and stands high above the River Tamar, near Gunnislake, which is part of the Cornish border. Although a glance at a map may suggest that the hill is a rough and uninteresting place, it is in fact quite fascinating and well worth a visit.

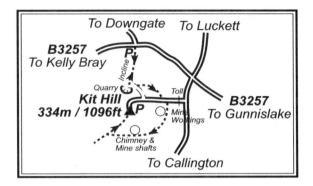

The town of Callington lies midway up on the south-western slopes, but this is not the best place to start and neither is the Tamar valley. Since there are no local footpaths, an ascent from low down on the slopes would simply be roadwalking alone and thus of little or no interest.

There are a number of parking places on and around the hill itself but, for the purposes of this walk, the best place to start is the one on the Kelly Bray to Gunnislake road, the B3257. This curves around the northern slopes of the ridge, close to the line of the old Kelly Bray railway that serviced the quarries and mines of Kit Hill. The parking place itself is well hidden. It lies up a track on the southern side of the road, just to the east of the Downgate road and between that junction and a lay-by on the opposite side of the road.

From the back of the car park and information board, a track runs up the hillside, actually an old quarry incline. Except for one change of slope midway, this embanked and disused tramway provides a steadily graded route up to the main granite quarry on the hill, which was in operation until 1955. Upon arrival, the mouth of the quarry can be seen across a trackway and a noticeboard inside gives further details.

Although the summit of the hill is easily attainable, our route now follows the waymarked trail around the slopes of the hill, which visits many of the points of interest. Marked by granite stones bearing an inscription of a chimney and green arrows, this now runs along the white roadway to the left. This ascends slightly before a green arrow points along a contouring path to the left. After traversing the gorse and heather hillside, the path reaches the hill road up to the summit in the vicinity of the old tin and wolfram mine; an information board in the car park opposite gives further details.

In the car park, opposite the noticeboard, the trail continues up the mine's prospecting trench, which uncovered four lodes, marked by cuttings off to the sides. The main one is deeper and is crossed by a footbridge. To the right, there is the gated entrance to the main level of the mine, whilst to the left there are fenced shafts. From the end of the trench, the green arrows continue to follow around the hill to the next chimney, which is surrounded by more fenced shafts and is a Victorian tin mine; again a noticeboard gives further information.

From here, the contouring, waymarked path continues along the slope before passing through a gate. Beyond this, the arrows turn up the hill on a small and narrow path climbing up through the heather and dwarf gorse to the prominent tower that marks the summit. The platform on which it sits forms the highest point, where the toposcopes are situated, whilst the trig point lies on another earthwork on the other side of the summit car park.

The descent back to the starting car park is much more direct and first drops down to the quarry. Follow the road down from the summit, continuing along it until, once it has swung around to the right, a small path starts to descend on the left. This leads down the right-hand side of the quarry to the track that reaches it from the hill road. The quarry entrance now lies just along to the left and the incline back down to the starting point begins opposite this.

Hensbarrow Beacon

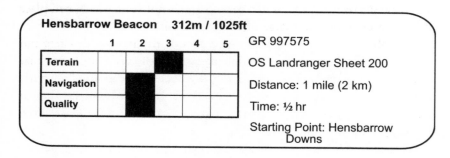

Hensbarrow Beacon   312m / 1025ft

	1	2	3	4	5
Terrain			■		
Navigation		■			
Quality		■			

GR 997575

OS Landranger Sheet 200

Distance: 1 mile (2 km)

Time: ½ hr

Starting Point: Hensbarrow Downs

The area to the north of St Austell is one of the main centres of the Cornish china clay industry. This white mineral, derived from granite, has a range of

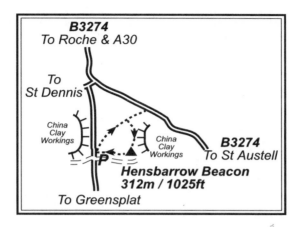

uses, including surfacing furniture as well as being used in the manufacture of ornamental china and toothpaste. The vast clay pits in this area and in a few other parts of Cornwall, plus those to the south-west of Dartmoor, make Britain one of the biggest china clay producers in the world.

No doubt, once upon a time, Hensbarrow Beacon was the highest point of a rolling stretch of granite moorland on the spine of Cornwall, known as the Hensbarrow Downs. Today, its summit is one of the few areas of green land left amidst a vast moonscape of white pits and spoil mountains created by the commercial operation to remove the china clay. Thus, Hensbarrow Beacon is now completely overshadowed by these white mountains, which, as each day goes by, climb ever more skyward as more waste is dropped onto their summits. However, on a warm summer's day, with blue sky overhead, the hill's 'summit' does not seem such a bad place after all, even amidst this large-scale destruction.

Inevitably, there are few places where a footpath can cross this area and such places that exist are occupied by roads. As such, any sort of a circular walk from valley level would necessitate a large amount of fairly uninteresting roadwalking. A small circuit can, however, be made close to the summit and the only place to start is the car park on the ridge above Roche on the Greensplat road.

Although a white gravel path leads straight to the summit from the car park, this is best left for the return. Instead, take off down the slope through a gate. The path then forks and here go right following a vehicle track underneath the telegraph lines and through the grass, heather and gorse that together vegetate this slope. The track bends to the right but still stays more or less under the wires, continuing towards the fence that bounds the foot of the spoil tip on the opposite slopes.

Crossing to this fence on a tiny path in the dwarf gorse and heather, the fenceline can then be followed back up the slope to a gate that gives access to the hilltop. The trig point and slightly higher boundary stone then both lie on the top of the mound ahead. The view to the north, despite the workings on both sides, over low land to the next ridge of rolling hills is good. In other directions, the spoil heaps hide any other views, although they themselves do form some interesting conical shapes. The spoil heap behind the car park can now be seen in its entirety and the white summit is visibly a good deal higher than the lower, natural-looking slopes that can be seen from the road.

The path westwards now leads directly back to the car park, close to a huge, wide road to the left, which links Littlejohn's Clay Works behind the car park with Gunheath Clay Works beyond the summit. For anyone who wishes to learn more about the industry and its history, there is a visitor centre at Wheal Martyn on the B3274 between here and St Austell. However, it is up here on the hilltops that the real work takes place, not on the wooded lower spoils that are available by the museum that the tourists see.

Carnmenellis

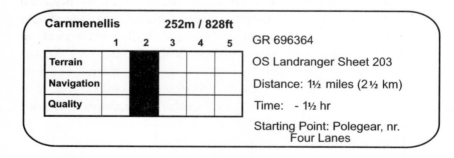

Carnmenellis		252m / 828ft			
	1	2	3	4	5
Terrain		■			
Navigation		■			
Quality		■			

GR 696364

OS Landranger Sheet 203

Distance: 1½ miles (2½ km)

Time: - 1½ hr

Starting Point: Polegear, nr. Four Lanes

Carnmenellis is not a hill that is climbed as an afternoon stroll or ramble, instead it can be seen as something of a collector's piece. No public rights

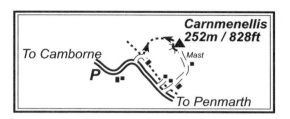

of way climb to the summit and the local farmers are not readily willing to allow walkers easy access to the summit. To make matters worse, the whole hill is surrounded by several little crofts and houses, making almost every side of the hill visible from a couple of different farms.

The summit is crowned by a radio mast and a water reservoir but the access road to these structures is clearly not intended for public use as it is marked private and runs through a farmyard. Most people who make the ascent do so on the north-west slopes and there is a convenient lay-by to park in on the road that runs along the south-western slopes of the hill. This road runs from Rame and Penmarth along to the B3297 Redruth to Helston road just to the south of Four Lanes. From the lay-by, walk south-eastwards towards Penmarth. Soon, the road bends sharply to the left and then back to the right. On the right-hand bend, a track ahead, which is a public right of way, leads up to the farm of Polgear Beacon. This shortly bends to the right in the direction of the buildings but before they are reached a track takes off to the left, leaving the right of way.

This track runs out onto the open hill and bends to the right. Another track, however, leads straight on and then this too bends to the right. Although a path runs straight on at the bend, follow around the bend and then turn left onto another small path in grass. This runs away, out of sight of the farm, above the field on the left. It then gradually starts to climb up towards a lower granite tor on the hillside. Here, the path passes through a gap in the fence and climbs up to the right through the grass, heather and dwarf gorse on the far side past a higher rock tor. The path then continues in this way up to the trig point and crosses the banked wall that continues up from the fence, before clambering over some further rocks close to the summit.

The view eastwards over Stithians Reservoir in the foreground towards Bodmin Moor really makes the climb to this summit more worthwhile, as otherwise it is a little overshadowed by the embanked reservoir and towering mast with its satellite dishes and other paraphernalia. The descent should be made by the same route to bring to an end an interesting but unfulfilling expedition.

Watch Croft

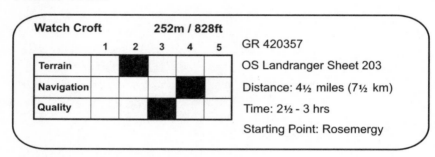

Watch Croft		252m / 828ft				
	1	2	3	4	5	GR 420357
Terrain		■				OS Landranger Sheet 203
Navigation				■		Distance: 4½ miles (7½ km)
Quality			■			Time: 2½ - 3 hrs
						Starting Point: Rosemergy

Watch Croft is the most southerly of England's separate summits and stands on the northern Cornish coast between St Ives and St Just in a wild and remote setting. It forms the highest point of the Land's End peninsula of Cornwall, which is the most westerly stretch of granite moorland in Cornwall and probably the least walked. Its moors and uplands are scattered with ancient standing stones, burial mounds and stone circles. In more recent times, the area was much exploited for its tin reserves, and the buildings and chimneys, which once hosted a thriving industry, now stand in solitude as stark reminders of the past.

There is a parking area by the remains of an old chimney and workshop alongside the B3306 St Ives to St Just road between the villages of Zennor to the east and Morvah to the west. From the right-hand end of the car park's seaward side, a small path cuts down through the scrubby vegetation and then crosses into a grass field over a stile. On the far side, it continues down towards some other mining ruins above Porthmoina Cove. From here, a small grass path climbs to the granite headland to the right, which is known as Bosigran Castle.

Continuing along the coast, the small path crosses through a semi-ruinous wall before meeting with the larger South West Coast Path, which has been running slightly inland through fields. Now merged

ABOVE: Brown Willy, the highest point of Bodmin Moor (Section 1), from the De Lank valley.

BELOW: The summit of Hensbarrow Beacon (Section 1) and the St Austell china clay workings.

ABOVE: Periton Hill and
eastern Exmoor from
Selworthy Beacon
(Section 2).

The limestone uplands around
Cheddar Gorge, as seen on the
Beacon Batch route (Section 2).

ABOVE: Golden Cap from above Seatown, as seen on the Hardown Hill route (Section 3).

One of the sea stacks at Ballard Point, as seen on the Nine Barrow Down route (Section 3).

ABOVE: The West Wiltshire Downs from near the summit of Win Green (Section 3).

BELOW: Leaden skies above the sharp summit ridge of Long Knoll (Section 3).

ABOVE: The Purbeck coastline at Kimmeridge, as seen on the Swyre Head route (Section 3).

BELOW: The South Downs near Ditchling Beacon (Section 4).

ABOVE: Malling Down and the western slopes of Cliffe Hill (Section 4).

BELOW: A wooded combe on the eastern slopes of Butser Hill (Section 4).

ABOVE: London and the North Downs from Leith Hill (Section 4),
the highest point in south-east England.

BELOW: A late afternoon view along the Greensand Ridge to Black Down
(Section 4), from Holmbury Hill.

ABOVE: A winter sunrise over the High Weald from Black Down (Section 4).

BELOW: The wooded slopes of Leith Hill (Section 4) from Holmbury Hill.

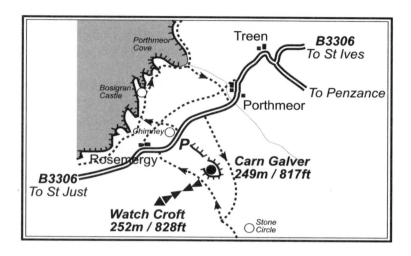

together, the path, becoming smaller and narrower, descends slightly above Haldrine Cove on the left before reaching an indistinct fork. Although the main path goes left, fork right on an improving path that climbs up over the next headland of Carn Veslan before dropping down once more and passing above the next, even narrower, cove of Great Zawn. After rounding the next headland, halfway down the seaward slope, a huge sheer drop into an inaccessible cove opens up immediately on the left of the path without warning; the path then continues towards the head of the larger Porthmeor Cove.

Before crossing the stream that flows down the small valley above the cove, look out for a path climbing up the valley to the right that branches off from the Coast Path. This small grassy path then ascends up the left-hand side of a sloping field to reach another path running along the hillside at a higher level. Still keeping straight ahead, the path then climbs up a small lane on the left-hand side of further fields out to the road above. The open hillside and rocks of Hannibal's Cairn now lie ahead but, instead of making towards them through the bracken, follow the road to the right. Opposite the signed entrance to Bosigran Farm on the right, a path takes off up the hillside to the left. This cuts a route through the grass, bracken and gorse up to the col on the skyline. Although the rocks and summit of Carn Galver on the right look very close, the intervening bracken is thick and difficult so, except in winter, it is not possible to reach them directly. Therefore, continue on the track, which soon enters a lane between banks and becomes increasingly vegetated, until it ends at a path running from left to right along in front of a fence.

On the moor to the left lies another chimney, as well as the stone circle of Nine Maidens, which is easily visited by turning left and then climbing up onto the top of that moor. However, our route turns to the right here and easily climbs up to the col between Carn Galver and Watch Croft. From here, a small path branches right to the rock tors on the summit of the former, which are easily surmounted to give a good panorama.

Although not far short, this is not the highest point of the moor, which lies a rough walk to the west on the summit of Watch Croft. Returning to the path at the col, follow it to the right to reach a dilapidated gate on the left. This boundary marks the edge of the open access moor and the rough ground on the far side is part of a private upland cattle pasture. Climbing the gate is not possible but the fence is easily crossed on either side by making use of the stone bank. Ahead, bar a few cattle tracks, the area is pathless and another barbed-wire fence, this time three-stranded, lies between here and the summit. To cross this second fence, walk on a bearing of 261° to a point where it is easily crossable. The summit, marked by a trig point and a shelter cairn, is then not much further ahead on more or less the same line.

A direct return to the car park from the summit is not feasible but it may be easily reached by returning to the dilapidated gate and turning left on the path, from which the car park is then in view.

Section 2 – The Somerset Hills and West Devon

River Axe from the Channel coast at Seaton to its source and then overland to the River Parrett. That waterway to the edge of the Somerset Levels and then their eastern margin to the Frome to Taunton railway line. The railway from there to Frome and then the River Frome to Bradford-on-Avon and River Avon to the Bristol Channel at Avonmouth. The coast from there to near Welcombe and then the Cornish–Devon county boundary along the River Tamar to the Channel coast at Plymouth. The coastline from there to Seaton.

NAME	HEIGHT	IN SECTION	IN ENGLAND	IN BRITAIN
Dunkery Beacon	519m / 1704ft	02 of 09	74 of 184	938 of 1552
Wills Neck	384m / 1261ft	03 of 09	108 of 184	1231 of 1552
Beacon Batch	325m / 1066ft	04 of 09	127 of 184	1335 of 1552
Staple Hill	315m / 1035ft	05 of 09	132 of 184	1350 of 1552
Selworthy Beacon	308m / 1012ft	06 of 09	136 of 184	1363 of 1552
Periton Hill	297m / 973ft	07 of 09	139 of 184	1376 of 1552
Christ Cross	261m / 857ft	08 of 09	157 of 184	1444 of 1552
Dundry Down	233m / 764ft	09 of 09	168 of 184	1480 of 1552

There is one summit on Dartmoor above 2,000ft that is described in *England's Highest Peaks*.

From the high, windswept summits of Exmoor and the hills around Tiverton to the rolling limestone Mendips, the scenery of Somerset and West Devon is very varied as a result of different successions of rocks of deposits. The oldest rocks date from the Devonian period, including some of the oldest in southern England, and the sequence continues all the way through to the Cretaceous, displaying some of the youngest rocks in the region, which were deposited whilst dinosaurs roamed the earth.

Hence, the region's geology begins in the Devonian. North America had collided into northern Europe, joining England and Scotland together and creating a chain of fold mountains, which were then eroded. Rivers washed these sediments out to an ocean to the south, whose northern shoreline fluctuated around Somerset and Bristol. The Devonian rocks of Somerset are more complicated than their Cornish contemporaries (see Section 1) as the advancing and retreating shoreline led to a record of alternating deposits. At times, the rocks deposited are similar to the marine deposits of Cornwall, at others the rocks bear similarities to the continental sediments laid down on what is called the Old Red Sandstone Continent to the north.

At the beginning of the Devonian, marine conditions prevailed over this area and the Lynton Beds (mudstones and sandstones) were deposited in shallow water. As the ocean retreated south, the continental Hangman Grits (coarse sandstones) and other conglomerates were laid down. Following this, the ocean transgressed north, flooding the area and allowing the Ilfracombe Beds (mudstones and limestones) to be deposited before again retreating back southwards to reveal deltaic conditions, forming the Morte Slates. A final return to continental facies heralded the Pickwell Down Sandstones before the last rocks of the Upper Devonian – the Upcott, Baggy and Pilton Beds (mudstones and sandstones) – were deposited once more under the ocean.

Hence, we reach the beginning of the Carboniferous. At this point, the ocean covering Cornwall and much of Devon spread northwards to cover all of England except some highland areas of the Midlands, known as St George's Land. Where the ocean was deepest, deposition of a sequence of mudstones and sandstones, known as the Culm Measures (see Section 1), followed directly on from the marine Devonian sequence in South Devon and West Somerset.

Further to the north, where the sea was shallower, the famous Carboniferous Mountain Limestones were deposited. The marine sequence began with a bed of shale, deposition of limestone only beginning in the Chadian or cycle three of the Dinantian (lower Carboniferous). In total, there were six cycles of the lower Carboniferous period with different rocks or beds being deposited in each. The Mountain

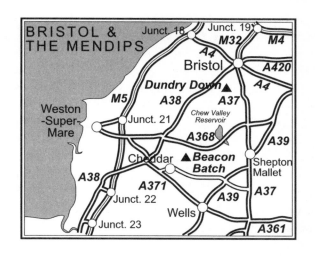

BRISTOL & THE MENDIPS

Junct. 18   Junct. 19
M32   M4
A4
Bristol   A420
Dundry Down▲   A4
M5   A38   A37
Junct. 21   Chew Valley Reservoir
Weston-Super-Mare   A368   A39
▲Beacon Batch   Shepton Mallet
Cheddar
A38   A371   A39   A37
Junct. 22   Wells
Junct. 23   A361

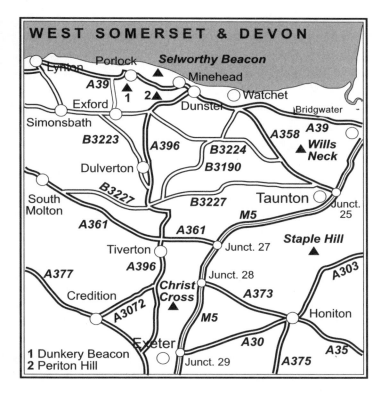

WEST SOMERSET & DEVON

Selworthy Beacon
Lynton   Porlock   Minehead
A39   ▲   Watchet
Exford   1   2▲   Dunster   Bridgwater
Simonsbath   A358   A39
B3223   A396   B3224   ▲Wills Neck
Dulverton   B3190
B3227   Taunton
South Molton   B3227   Junct. 25
A361   M5
A361   Staple Hill
Tiverton   Junct. 27   ▲
A377   A396   Junct. 28   A303
Credition   Christ Cross   A373
A3072   ▲   Honiton
M5
Exeter   A30   A35
Junct. 29   A375

1 Dunkery Beacon
2 Periton Hill

Limestones were deposited in cycles two, three, four and five, in the mid to late part of the Dinantian. The limestones are generally extremely pure, about 98 per cent calcium carbonate, which gives them a very white colour, in contrast to the deeper yellow colour of the oolitic limestones in places such as the Cotswolds (Section 5) and Dundry Down.

However, the warm shallow shelf-sea in which the limestone was deposited was not to last. A river delta encroached from the north bringing about completely different conditions, which led to the deposition of a cyclical succession of limestone, shales, siltstones, sandstones and thin coal seams. This was followed in the upper Carboniferous period, when deltaic conditions were firmly established, by the rocks of the Millstone Grit Facies (grits, shales and sandstones) and above that the Coal Measures. Although the deposits higher than the limestone have since been eroded in Devon, they still exist in the nearby South Wales coalfield where a syncline has saved them from nature's erosive forces.

The Carboniferous came to an end at a time of massive geological upheaval. The ocean separating the Old Red Sandstone continent from the only other landmass at the time – Gondwanaland – closed. This formed one huge supercontinent called Pangaea. The crumpling over southern Britain formed a large syncline, known as the central Devon syncline, with its centre in the Holsworthy area. This is where the Carboniferous Culm Measures are exposed and, northwards, the ground rises onto the increasingly older Devonian rocks that form Exmoor and the Quantocks.

The other effect of this mountain building episode, called the Amorican orogeny, was the intrusion of a granite mass under south-west England. This occurred later in the orogeny, probably in the early Permian, and pushed up the Mendips in an anticline. Amorican volcanics are also responsible for the igneous rocks on Start Point, which are formed like those on the Lizard (see Section 1). The granite batholith is exposed on the surface on Dartmoor, the most easterly of the south-west's granite moorlands, where the ground rises above 2,000ft (610m) at the summit of High Willhays.

Hot saline solutions from the cooling granite were forced under pressure, as described in Section 1, into cracks in the limestone (tension faults). In these cracks, the pressure reduced and consequently the solution cooled, allowing many minerals contained in it to be deposited in veins.

These minerals include galena (lead sulphide), fluorspar (calcium fluoride), barite (barium sulphate), dolomite (calcium magnesium carbonate), calcite (calcium carbonate), witherite (barium carbonate), pyromorphite (lead chloro-phosphate), quartz (silica), pyrite (iron sulphide) and sphalerite (zinc sulphide), some formed by metasomatism – reaction of the solutions with limestone.

These veins vary in size but are generally quite narrow, deep and long. Other deposits, known as lenticles, occur between limestone beds as lateral precipitates. As explained below, the limestone plateau of the Mendips is very dry and, as such, it was not settled. However, mining villages, such as Priddy and Charterhouse, were set up to exploit the lead and zinc in the mineral veins. The mining and dressing process is the same as that used for cassiterite (tin ore) in Cornwall (detailed in Section 1).

Lead ore, or galena, is, however, smelted in a different way from cassiterite. Galena is lead sulphide and, thus, the smelting of the dressed ore is a two-stage process. Firstly it is necessary to oxidise (burn) the galena thus:

Galena + oxygen → lead oxide + sulphur dioxide

Following oxidation, carbon, carbon monoxide or simply more galena was added to reduce ('de-oxidise') the lead oxide:

Lead oxide + **galena** → **lead** + sulphur dioxide

Zinc is obtained from its ore, sphalerite (zinc sulphide), in a similar way. Lead smelting was originally done in small furnaces where the lead ran out from between the dross (waste) into a sumpter pot, from which it was poured into moulds. In the larger smelt mills, reverberatory furnaces were introduced which could cope with larger amounts of lead, as they were bigger and designed to be run continuously, fuelled by a coal or coke fire. In total, it could be expected to obtain 87 tonnes of lead from 100 tonnes of galena. However, since an average vein contained only about 5 to 10 per cent galena, it was necessary to mine about 15 tonnes of rock to obtain just 1 tonne of lead. The large costs involved in mining this relatively low-grade ore, creating vast amounts of spoil, and the large cost of smelting led ultimately to the demise of the industry due to competition from cheaper Spanish imports.

Although limestone itself is a non-porous rock due to its crystalline character, it is broken by horizontal planes and vertical joints. This means that vertical erosion can weather the rock into the clints and grikes of limestone pavements and that potholes can form. Lateral erosion can also form caves, with their bases along the horizontal planes. The lime-rich soils give rise to verdant green pastures, even though the soil is quite dry as rainwater sinks immediately underground. This means that the Mendip villages rest on a small bench around the foot of the hills, where the subterranean streams reappear into daylight. Cheddar is possibly the most famous of these scarp-foot settlements and, although it was once thought that its famous gorge was a collapsed cave, today it is widely believed to have been carved by water as a surface feature. There are, however, caves in the Mendip Hills, such as those at Wookey Hole, near Wells, and at Cheddar, as well as those seen on the Beacon Batch route.

In the Triassic period, storms eroded the summits of the Mendips and vast torrents of water carried the limestone material from the summits down the slopes of the dome to the Vale of Taunton to form the Triassic marls of that area and the bench feature around the foot of the Mendip scarp. This erosion exposed the Old Red Sandstones on the highest summits, including Beacon Batch, where wet, rough moorlands, akin to parts of Exmoor, prevail, in complete contrast to the surrounding dry, green and verdant pastures on the limestone.

The Triassic period was followed by the Jurassic, and once again a shallow sea covered England. The deposition of limestones then began again, although this time it was the honey-coloured oolitic limestones of Bath and the Cotswolds (see Section 5). These rocks form a ridge running south from the Cotswolds through Chipping Sodbury and Radstock to the Dorset Coast. Dundry Down is a Jurassic monolith formed in the same way as Bredon Hill (see Section 5).

By the end of the Jurassic, Britain was, once again, above the waves. However, an ocean was then to return in the Cretaceous period when the Lower Greensand rock, the Gault Clay and the Upper Greensand strata were deposited (see Section 4). These sediments are, in more eastern areas (such as Section 3), mostly overtopped by the chalk but here they form the uppermost strata due to the erosion of the higher strata by the uplift of western Britain in the Tertiary period as the Atlantic ocean started to form. The Upper Greensands and Gault Clay of the Blackdown Hills form part of the westernmost extent of the Cretaceous strata.

Hence, the rocks were deposited and the land was generally shaped –

bar the erosion in the arctic tundra conditions that existed across southern England during the ice ages. Devonian Old Red Sandstones form the high moorlands of Exmoor, the Brendon Hills and the Quantocks, forming the summits of Selworthy Beacon, Dunkery Beacon, Periton Hill and Wills Neck. The deep-ocean Carboniferous and Devonian strata extend around the edges of Dartmoor through the summit of Christ Cross into South Devon. These red Devonian sandstones, should not, however, be confused with the Permian and Triassic New Red Sandstones that form the cliffs around Sidmouth. The Mendips rise as a limestone upland, like a miniature version of the White Peak (Volume 2), to their highest point on Beacon Batch, with the Jurassic limestones outcropping on Dundry Down just a few miles to the north. Finally, the youngest sandstones of the Cretaceous period form the wooded summits of the Blackdown Hills in the east of the section, the highest of which is Staple Hill.

Accommodation

Both the north and south coasts in this section are lined with tourist towns. Minehead, Clevedon and Weston-super-Mare on the northern Bristol Channel coast, and Sidmouth, Exmouth, Exeter, Dawlish, Dartmouth, Torbay, Paignton and Teignmouth on the southern coast. In between, towns like Crediton and Tiverton nestle amongst the sandstone hills between Dartmoor and Exmoor. On Exmoor itself, there is a lot of accommodation available in villages and farmhouses, as well as in the popular town of Lynmouth and its slightly more old-fashioned neighbour Porlock further east along the coast. Around the Mendips, villages and towns like Cheddar, Glastonbury and Wells are all popular tourist destinations. For the Blackdown Hills, Taunton or even Lyme Regis would be a good base and in the latter case, the western hills in the Wessex Downs (Section 3) surround the town. There are youth hostels at Ilfracombe, Lynton, Exford, Minehead, Quantock Hills, Street, Cheddar, Bath and Bristol on or near to the north coast, with Plymouth, Salcombe, Maypool, Exeter and Beer on the southern coast and Dartington, Steps Bridge and Okehampton on or near Dartmoor.

Dunkery Beacon, Selworthy Beacon and Periton Hill

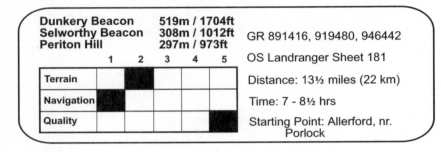

	1	2	3	4	5
Terrain		■			
Navigation	■				
Quality					■

Dunkery Beacon 519m / 1704ft
Selworthy Beacon 308m / 1012ft
Periton Hill 297m / 973ft

GR 891416, 919480, 946442

OS Landranger Sheet 181

Distance: 13½ miles (22 km)

Time: 7 - 8½ hrs

Starting Point: Allerford, nr. Porlock

This walk is Exmoor's very own 'Three Peaks Walk', although it should in no way be compared to the marathon walk in the Yorkshire Dales, which links the summits of Ingleborough, Whernside and Pen-y-ghent. It seems most logical to link these three hills on the north-eastern side of Exmoor together as they form a cradle around the villages to the east of Porlock, such as Allerford and Selworthy. This is one of the toughest walks in the book, but it is also the one that I personally rate most highly because of its spectacular views and largely unspoilt and beautiful landscape.

The best place to start is the small and pretty village of Allerford, from where it is possible to make a good wide circuit over these hills without any repetition. The main road into the village is signposted off the A39 between Porlock and Minehead, although the village can also be reached from Porlock through Bossington. There is a car park in the village with room for nine or ten cars. The car park has its own toilets and lies down the Bossington road, opposite the village forge.

Begin by walking along to the packhorse bridge and ford in the middle of the village, where the road bends right to run out to the A39. Cross the bridge and follow the lane on the far side that runs along the hillside past further houses in the upper part of the village. When this road bends to the right, leave it for a track that continues straight ahead, making a gradual ascent of the hillside. It soon enters a wood, where the route crosses straight over a crosstracks. This is followed by another track that branches off to the left close to the far edge of the trees. This is signposted to Selworthy Beacon and the route now follows this on an unremitting climb to the top of the wood. Ignoring any tracks or paths running to the left or right, the more open hillside above is reached through a gate and above that there is a junction of paths.

Here, a right turn should be made on the most right-handed of the two

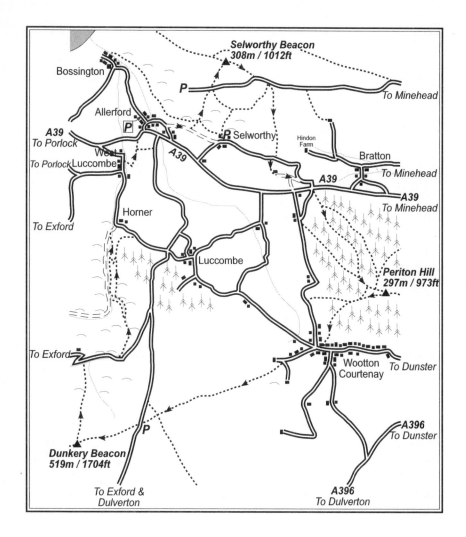

paths, which reaches a further junction in a matter of yards. Continue straight ahead along a small grassy path through a stand of trees and past a bench, out to the road that climbs up from Minehead. A right turn leads along to the point where a track branches off to the left up the final gently inclined slopes to the trig point on the summit. From here, the seawards view is very good. As well as the islands of Flat Holm and Steep Holm in the Bristol Channel to the north, the coast of South Wales is clearly visible, stretching from the industrial heartlands around Port Talbot through

Carmarthenshire and past the golden sands at Pendine to the first peninsula of the Pembrokeshire coastline. Landwards, the Quantocks appear prominently but the bulk of Dunkery Hill rather limits the view out over Exmoor.

Beyond the summit, the trackway continues on across the heathy moor before forking. Take the left fork and follow it down until it comes close to the road, at which point branch right to the road on a path between gorse thickets. Slanting across the road, a track on the far side continues the descent above Selworthy Combe down on the right. Going straight over a crosstracks, the inbye is soon reached and the lane continues onwards, banked and hemmed in by hedges on both sides. In due course, it reaches a small road running along from Selworthy at Dean's Cross. Still following the signposts to Dunster, go right (actually straight ahead) and then left (again actually straight ahead).

An even narrower leafy lane now proceeds down the slope to the house at East Lynch, from where the bridleway follows its access down below the house to some farm buildings. Here, the path branches left, above the buildings, and then drops back down to the road, which is then followed onwards and out to the same lane further along (ignore a track that branches right down the slope midway from the farm). This road can then be followed ahead and down along the bottom of Little Headon Plantation to Headon Cross on the A39.

Ahead lies Periton Hill. This is completely different in character from either Selworthy or Dunkery Beacon in that its slopes are almost entirely wooded and the only open space is on and around the summit. The ascent begins by following a path on the left bank of the road ahead, which, when it enters the trees, is signposted to Minehead and Dunster. Ignoring any tracks to the left or right, keep straight on up the slopes and through the broadleaved woodland on the lower slopes. Higher up, the track starts to level off and runs along the right-hand side of the ridge ahead as the trees turn more to conifers. It soon regains the ridge after a long level stretch, before then running along the left-hand side of the ridge. Soon after, it begins to climb again and, after joining with a track from the right, enters more scrubby woodland in the National Trust-owned area beyond a squat cairn that bears the byelaws. The summit is now close at hand and the track bends left to it alongside a beech hedge. Ignoring a track to the right to Wootton Courtenay, the trig point is reached in the bank on the right after a small and gentle ascent and is opposite an unsafe wooden bench.

The trig point, however, does not quite mark the highest point. This is reached by turning sharply back right on a second track signposted to Wootton Courtenay; the high point is to be found just before the track forks. Take the right fork on a track, which is signposted as a bridleway and starts to descend gradually, before joining with the other earlier track to Wootton Courtenay that previously branched off the ridge track. Beyond this, the track soon starts to emerge from the wood itself and runs high above a deep combe down on the left. Now the descent also begins and quickly, without any deviation, the track meets the main road by the hotel in the small village of Wootton Courtenay.

A right turn on this road soon leads along to the edge of the village where the road splits three ways. Take the leftmost road, which crosses over the valley and passes a number of large and substantial houses en route. At the far side, under the slopes of Dunkery Hill, it swings to the left but here a path climbs up ahead and past the National Trust sign into the wooded lower slopes. After a more level stretch, it finally emerges from the top of the wood and, after running through a thick section of gorse, it gently climbs over the heathery moor on a well-graded path up to the top of the shoulder ahead. Again, a more level section is reached before a further gentle climb up to the moorland road.

Straight across, the track continues, although it is now much wider due to the many people who stroll up from the car park to the highest point on Exmoor. Soon, the large summit cairn appears on the skyline and the track then climbs steadily up to it. Although the seaward view is not as impressive as on Selworthy Beacon, the general panorama is better, with nothing now blocking the view over Exmoor and south towards Dartmoor. The toposcope also details the towns and villages that can be seen along the Bristol Channel coast to the north and over in South Wales, where the Sugar Loaf is prominent.

The descent begins by following the grassier footpath that runs north from the summit. Various paths are crossed on the descent but soon our path nears the top of the inbye as the deepening combe on the right becomes wooded. Before reaching the field gate, but after a crosstracks, fork right down into the trees along a steepening path that finishes by dropping down a series of hairpins to the road in the East Water Valley, after fording the beck.

Horner now lies to the right and the route to it begins by following this road. It soon passes a footbridge on the right and then a more open grassy parking area. However, just before the road itself fords the beck, take off to the left down an initially broad track. This begins on the left-hand bank of the beck in the increasingly narrow and confined valley with its occasional sandstone craglets. As the valley sides close in, the path begins to criss-cross the stream on bridges, each with its original ford alongside. In total, there are four bridges to be crossed, after which the path follows the left-hand bank. Beyond this, ignore any fords on the right and follow the path on the left bank until the track finally crosses a fifth bridge back to the far bank.

The valley, although very deep and wooded, has now widened out a little and the track can take a straighter route. However, interest can be added by taking a traverse path along the slopes of the right-hand hill. This is signposted 'Nature Trail' and, after an initial short ascent, takes a fairly level course along a narrow ledge high up on the hillside above the chattering beck. Soon, the route is running high above the valley in the trees and it passes the steep, wooded valley of Yeals Combe, which drops into the main valley on the far side. After this, the Nature Trail turns sharply back to the right up the slope and, here, our route turns to the left down the hairpins.

Although there is a shortcut, it is much more preferable – as well as helping to minimise erosion damage – to ignore the loose direct path and instead follow the easily graded hairpins to the valley bottom below. At this point, stay on the near bank of the beck, which has now been swollen almost to the proportions of a river, and continue down by its side to reach a gate into a field. A little further down on the left, there is a footbridge back over the stream and this should be crossed before continuing down through the field to another gate at the far end.

This gate gives access to the trackway that has been following the left-hand side of the valley, which now promptly crosses the beck on a stone-arched bridge; the hamlet of Horner is now not much further. On the edge of the hamlet, the road is met on a bend opposite the local tearoom, which, if timed right, would make an ideal stopping place for a well-deserved cream tea! (Alternatively, there is another tearoom at Allerford.) Straight ahead, the road now leads down and through the village before passing the campsite on the far side. After passing a packhorse bridge on the left, the road crosses the beck itself and enters the village of West Luccombe.

After passing the first and only house on the right, a more open grassy area is reached. A bridleway leaves to the right, fording the beck. However, there is also a footbridge a little further on and both options lead onto a trackway running down a lane between fields. After turning briefly back towards Dunkery, the lane then makes a very sharp left bend to continue its northwards progression out to the A39 near Allerford; ignore a branching track on the right to Piles Mill. On the busy and narrow road, a right turn leads up the few hundred yards to where the road into Allerford branches off to the left by the tearoom. The car park is then only a short distance further on and around to the left.

Wills Neck

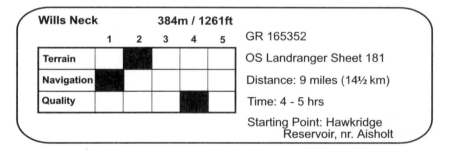

Wills Neck		384m / 1261ft			
	1	2	3	4	5
Terrain		■			
Navigation	■				
Quality				■	

GR 165352

OS Landranger Sheet 181

Distance: 9 miles (14½ km)

Time: 4 - 5 hrs

Starting Point: Hawkridge Reservoir, nr. Aisholt

Towards the southern end of their long north-west to south-east-running ridge, the Quantock Hills, to the north of Taunton, climb to their highest point on the moorland summit of Wills Neck. Although there are two possible parking areas close to the summit itself, using these would detract from the feeling of elevation that is best experienced by beginning at its foot.

This walk begins at the car park at Hawkridge Reservoir, which lies on the eastern side of the ridge. There is a large car park next to the Aisholt to Bridgwater road that runs along the reservoir's southern shore. Begin by walking west along this road to where it meets the road running north from Taunton through Kingston St Mary. Following this road to the right,

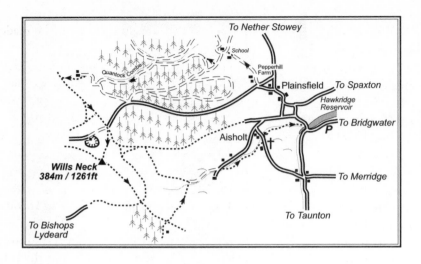

it crosses the upper part of the reservoir before climbing across the face of the slope on the far side. On the top, it swings to the right at a first junction and then back left at the second to run into the hamlet of Plainsfield. After turning again to the right at a third junction, take the next road on the left, which continues on over a couple of streams to a further junction and small car park on the edge of the hamlet.

On the far side of this road, a track leads up to the buildings at Pepperhill Farm. In the yard, the bridleway swings to the right outside the fence and around the front of the farmhouse before climbing slightly through a wood to reach more open parkland beyond. Keeping more or less straight on over this field, the track then climbs further to another gate that this time leads into the grounds of a school. Now off the farm, the roadway continues past an ornamental entrance on the left before descending slightly through a wood where it becomes a rough path. At the foot, a left turn leads past more school buildings on the right until the road bends to the right to Adscombe.

Here, keep more or less straight on up a track, through rhododendron bushes, that is signposted to Keeper's Combe. It enters the forestry plantations that clothe the lower eastern Quantock slopes over a filled-in cattle grid, after which a right turn should be made. This track now takes a more level course close to the lower edge of the plantation, crossing various tracks descending the slope from up on the left. Eventually, though, it meets a larger forestry road that comes in at an acute angle from the left. Although the track keeps straight on, a right turn should be made here down into the valley above Adscombe.

Ignoring a bridge into the campsite on the right, the forestry road keeps on up the left-hand side of the valley, running underneath electricity lines, to a house where the road ends. Here, there is an alternative parking area on the right but our route goes left into Quantock Combe, heading for St David's Well. The track now starts to rise again as the wooded valley narrows and becomes increasingly confined. Ignoring any tracks climbing up the hillside to the left, follow this track as it makes its way up the left-hand side of the stream becoming ever closer to it. After passing a grassy area on the right, the stone enclosure over the spring known as St David's Well is reached on the left.

You are now very close to the top of the wood and soon the track leaves it for a more open, bracken-covered hillside, with rhododendron thickets to the left, as it climbs out of the top of the valley. After some ascent, the trackway ends on a higher track that runs left to right. The ridge is now nearly underfoot and a right turn leads up to the entrance to the gardens of Quantock Farm. Here, the bridleway turns to the left up the slope, outside the gardens, before turning back to the right above the fence along the edge of the first field. After passing the house, the track continues to a small gate into a higher field half right. The bridleway now follows the left-hand beech hedge up to a gate giving access to the track along the ridge, which follows a beech-lined avenue.

Following this track to the left, it continues along its avenue to the car park at Triscombe Stone. Here, a road climbs up Cockercombe to the ridge from Plainsfield down to the left, and then becomes a rougher track as it drops down to the right to Triscombe itself. The final ascent now begins on the far side of the car park where the track forks. Take the right branch, which ascends to a higher level and continues to the foot of the final slope where it again forks. This time, take the left-hand track, which climbs across the slope and leads directly to the trig point above. Although the Ordnance Survey believe the highest point to be on the next small hummock to the right, from all viewpoints the trig point certainly does appear to overtop all else by a small margin. The view is spectacular in all directions, with the sea visible in at least two different places and the mudflats of the Bristol Channel being particularly evident. Also prominent are the reactor buildings at the nuclear power station of Hinkley Point.

To begin the descent, continue southwards along the ridge, following it as it descends to a beech woodland. Ignoring paths to the left and the right, follow the track down the left-hand side of the wood to the far end where there is a gate and stile. Rather than crossing the fence, turn left down a path on its nearside, which soon becomes increasingly apparent on the ground. With the descent now steepening, the path swings to the right and then reaches a stile into the inbye. In this thistle-covered field, the right of way slants off half left, down the slope, to a gate in the bottom right-hand corner of the field. This leads into a rough lane on the left bank of the stream, which then leads down to the top of the public road in the valley above Aisholt.

Soon after fording the stream and passing through a gate on the right on a signposted byway, the route leaves the road to take the field path to Aisholt. This goes off on the left through an unmarked and collapsing black metal gate. The path then sticks to the bottom of this large field to reach the back of the hamlet of Aisholt. Although the exit from the field is not immediately apparent, a gate can be reached by dropping down the bank on the left over a badger sett, before going along right to the road, which is met at the foot of the church tower that has been visible across the field.

To the left, the road now descends steeply towards the valley floor but, just before it reaches it, another signposted bridleway turns off to the right along the back of and slightly above a half-timbered house. Following the valley around to the right, this track then leads along the bottom of the nature reserve of Aisholt Wood, managed by the Somerset Wildlife Trust. Soon after that, it crosses the stream and then splits. Take the right branch, which follows a level course just above the valley floor, along to the road by the reservoir where the outward route is rejoined close to the reservoir car park.

Beacon Batch

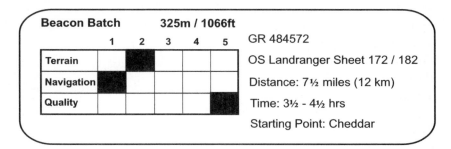

Beacon Batch		325m / 1066ft				
	1	2	3	4	5	GR 484572
Terrain		■				OS Landranger Sheet 172 / 182
Navigation	■					Distance: 7½ miles (12 km)
Quality					■	Time: 3½ - 4½ hrs
						Starting Point: Cheddar

Beacon Batch is the highest point of the Mendips and lies on the tract of moorland known as Black Down on the northern fringe of the hills. Nestling at the foot of its slopes lies the village of Cheddar, world famous for its cheese and gorge. Behind the village, the gorge extends as a massive rift in the limestone hillside with its vertical and, in some places, overhung walls rising for hundreds of feet above the rocky bottom through which the public road winds tortuously.

In terms of scenery, there is only one place to start this walk and that is the village of Cheddar. In summer, its bustling streets are overflowing with the tourists that flock here and parking in the village may be understandably difficult. The best place to park is near to the public toilets on the Draycott road out of the village. This pay and display car park is the most convenient, although late arrivals may have to begin from further afield at the western side of the village close to the reservoir.

From the car park, walk eastwards to a small roundabout where a right turn should be made to cross the swift-flowing River Yeo that emerges from a cave into daylight by the entrance to Gough's Cave a few hundred yards upstream. On the other side of the river, by the first café, a further right turn should be made up a small lane named The Lippiatt. This climbs uphill through the narrow confines between houses on the congested hillside. Soon though, another little lane takes off to the left, which forks behind the main block of houses. Taking the left branch, the signposted bridleway then turns to the left again in front of the gates of the house ahead.

Continuing the ascent, the path climbs around the edge of this property to reach the lookout tower at the top of Jacob's Ladder. Of course, those who have visited Cox's Cave can ascend directly up the 'ladder', saving

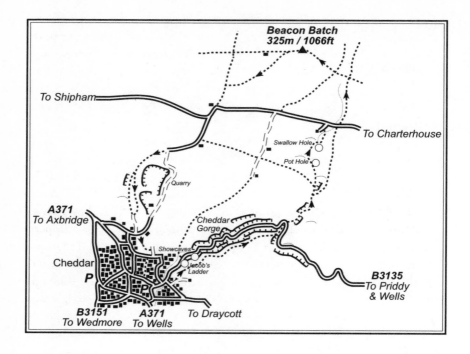

themselves the extra walk. To the right, the path continues past the information board and on up the gentler slope. Occasional limestone bluffs in the trees on the left offer views over the edge and down the wooded slopes to the gorge, whose walls have not yet become truly vertical. However, especially as the climb progresses, it is best to keep pets and children under close control.

As the path climbs, the gorge becomes much more pronounced. When a more open area is reached, it is the retrospective view that captures the attention with the Somerset Levels laid out on the other side of Cheddar Reservoir before the Welsh mountains. However, it is the monolithic hills of Glastonbury Tor and Nyland Hill that steal the scene to the south.

Eventually, the path splits close to the highest section of cliff. Those of a nervous disposition and who believe discretion to be the better part of valour should sneak off ahead on the track through the bracken. However, it is far better to walk left and out along the edge as close as you dare to the very highest section of the cliff. That said, if you can steel yourself, turn left slightly down the slope to a narrow promontory that runs out between two gullies. From the gorge, this appears to be an overhung spire and its narrow grassy top, about one yard wide, supports vertical drops for well over a hundred feet on three sides. If that's not enough, then, lying on your stomach and peering over the edge, you can see matchbox cars disappearing beneath you around a horseshoe bend on the road far below. Obviously, this is quite precarious so exercise extreme caution at all times.

All routes (with the exception of straight on from the end of the rock promontory!) rejoin and continue to follow the waymarked route of the Gorge Walk, which we have been following since the top of Jacob's Ladder. Continue along using the waymarkers and down through a wood to reach the road near the top of the gorge. Take care on the descent, however, as the polished limestone path under the trees remains treacherously slippery and greasy.

The road is crossed at a small car parking area on a bend. Opposite, and slightly to the right, a path leads on and into the nature reserve. Although hidden to motorists by trees, the main valley continues up here and this route will now follow it to its source high on Black Down. The lower section of the nature reserve is called Black Rocks and, beyond the trees, a lime kiln and old grassy quarry are passed on the left before reaching a gate. Here, the valley splits but stay on this side of the gate and follow the left-hand combe.

The path soon climbs steeply up and out of the valley but before it does so a gate on the right gives access to a permitted path that continues up the dry valley. The route now enters the Somerset Wildlife Trust's reserve at Long Wood, some of which qualifies as ancient woodland. Although the nature trail soon takes off to the right, keep on up the shady and cool valley path. The first point of interest is a black hole on the left. This is one of the entrances to the valley's extensive cave system and below its locked gated entrance and derelict winch, some rough steps descend into the blackness.

Continuing up the valley, it is now not far until the woodland echoes to the sound of tumbling water for the first time since Cheddar. In a dark pool, the purling stream disappears underground, to reappear as the River Yeo by Gough's Cave. A few yards further on, on the right bank, a raised cover marks another cave opening. This is the dry entrance used by explorers and through the narrow hole in the cover, through which a cooling breeze escapes, all is black, apart from a glinting metal mechanism at the top of the shaft.

For the next few yards, the path continues on the left bank but then crosses over a bridge and climbs steeply out of the valley to enter a field at the top of the wood. Follow the field edge to the left until a trackway leads out on the left and over the beck to the dead-end road that leads to Lower Farm; a right turn leads out to the small Charterhouse to Shipham road.

Ahead lie the final slopes of Beacon Batch and a path leads up them just a short distance to the right and back over the stream. The path follows the wooded course of the stream along the left-hand edge of a field to its top. Here, the path splits but, instead of crossing into the wood, keep ahead into the next field. At this point the wood finishes and the path follows the curve of the ever-decreasing trickle to a stile at the top above its source. Just over this stile, a track leads left and out onto the open moor of Black Down. Here, keep pretty much straight on and up to the summit trig point with its three tumuli.

From the summit, both Severn bridges are in view, while Bristol lies tucked away behind the green mass of Dundry Down beside the huge expanse of the Chew Valley Reservoir. Beyond that, the dark bulk of the Cotswold scarp runs northwards past Wotton-under-Edge to Cheltenham. Westwards, the Somerset Levels appear to blend invisibly into the Welsh mountains, while to the south the River Parrett curves its way towards the Quantocks and the bulk of Exmoor beyond.

The descent route begins as a dead straight path running west-south-west from the summit. Although invisible until it is reached, a slanting crosstracks is found shortly and a left turn here leads along a track that is atrociously boggy in places to reach the other tracks and the top of the inbye at a gate. Through this, a joint path leads across the field and past two large limestone blocks to the road at Tyning's Farm.

Here, follow the road straight ahead for about a hundred yards until it turns to the right at Tyning's Cross. Rather than turning right on the road, keep going straight ahead down a surfaced lane marked as unsuitable for motor vehicles. This passes Ashridge Farm, a light airfield and a semi-derelict motor-racing track before reaching the end of the tarmac at the upper entrance to Batts Coombe Quarry.

At this point, the bridleway continues down the green lane ahead, with a steep descent over the dreaded polished limestone cobbles under trees. After a while, the lane reaches a gate, through which the main track should be left for a path on the left that initially runs parallel. This drops steeply along the left-hand margin of the wood before splitting. Stay on the same line and follow the edge of the trees down the hill, even more steeply, to join with a larger track that leads out to a small lane at Hamfield, a suburb of Cheddar.

The starting point is now not too distant and it is best reached by turning to the left along this road. Just past a cottage on the right, an unsignposted path crosses the wall on the right and slants across the field ahead to the left, before entering a narrow, fenced, mown lane. This leads through the allotments before reaching a wider lane that, to the right, leads out to another road. Here, go slightly right over the imaginatively named Gardener's Close before turning left into a housing estate just before the road narrows by the Gardener's Arms. This residential road leads onwards and across a staggered crossroads before bending to the right. Here, go straight on and down a short alley that leads out to the Axbridge road. The mini-roundabout at the junction with the Draycott road is now only a short distance to the left past the toilets.

Staple Hill

Staple Hill						315m / 1035ft
	1	2	3	4	5	GR 240167
Terrain	█					OS Landranger Sheet 193
Navigation	█					Distance: 6½ miles (10 km)
Quality	█					Time: 3 - 3½ hrs
						Starting Point: Castle Neroche

To the south of Taunton, the Blackdown Hills attain their highest point at the summit of Staple Hill. Despite having a good road network, the area has many non-existent or blocked footpaths and this makes a circular route to the summit almost impossible. The route described here involves a good deal of roadwalking, although it is possible to park to the west of the summit close to the Yarcombe to Taunton road.

This walk starts at the fortified hilltop known as Castle Neroche. Here, there is a small car park on a side road just off the road that crosses the hill

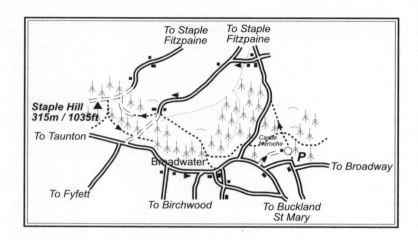

between Buckland St Mary and Staple Fitzpaine. From the car park, enter the wood by a path in the far corner and cross over a track just inside its edge to reach a noticeboard that details the site's history. At this point, a bench to the right overlooks possibly the finest view of the day which encompasses the Quantocks, Mendips and Brecon Beacons.

Our route begins by descending these slopes by a track slightly to the left. Ignoring a left fork into a farmyard, this track drops steeply down the ridge alongside the earthworks on the left. Soon a junction of paths is reached, where the route takes the furthest left of the tracks directly ahead. This green lane, which is wet in places, continues on and down to meet the road crossing the ridge just opposite Lane End Farm.

The first section of roadwalking now follows and this begins by following the road straight ahead down the slope. It passes a chapel on a small hill to the right before reaching a farm on the edge of the village of Staple Fitzpaine. Here there is a crossroads and the lane to the left leads across a small valley and then up the opposite slopes, joining with another lane from further down in the village.

Passing a farm on the right, the lane climbs the slopes ahead. The banks of the lane are full of pretty flowers and interesting plants. It passes through a small copse before reaching its end at the next habitation, Mount Fancy Farm. Still climbing, the track then leads on past the buildings and towards the bottom of the wood. However, before the wood, a gate and stile on the right give access into a rough field.

This path, actually the Neroche Millennium Walk, crosses an initial wet patch before working its way through bracken to the far side, where it enters the wood over a stile by another gate. The forestry road beyond is quite pleasant and grassy to begin with but later becomes rough and wet in places. After a while, it meets another track that has started only a short distance to the left. Turning to the right, the route follows this track, which continues the traverse along the hillside and past a set of old stables to reach a track descending the hill at an acute angle.

The ascent back up onto the ridge now begins in earnest. Turning sharply to the left on this bridleway, the route climbs up and across the slope, meeting with another bridleway joining from the left at the top. The summit plateau has now been reached although the very highest point remains hidden amongst the trees. Continuing straight on, a widening in the road is found and, here, the route turns off the road into the trees. The moss-covered trig point lies about a hundred yards into the wood on a bearing of 226° (half left) and is reached unexpectedly as it is so well camouflaged; it is surrounded by a much more visible ring of small pebbles that have been left by previous intrepid visitors.

The ridge walk back to the car park begins by walking back out to the forest road and then following that back along to the right. Very shortly, a bridleway turns off to the right and this should be followed to a gate on the left. Here, a smaller track on the left runs parallel to the bridleway but on the other side of the bank. This track soon swings to the left and continues along inside but close to the edge of some more scrubby woodland.

Before too long, it reaches a crosstracks with the track that climbs up the slope from Mount Fancy Farm and this other track should now be followed out to the right to the road on the ridge. The second stretch of road-walking now commences by following this road to the left along the edge of the wood where you can enjoy fine southwards views through gaps in the hedge.

It passes a couple of farms and three roads take off to the right before the main road bends around to the right where the Taunton road goes off down the scarp to the left. Not far around this bend, a signposted bridleway takes off to the left down a concrete road. Follow this back up to the farm buildings within the fortified summit of Castle Neroche. After passing through the sheds, the outward route is rejoined close to the car park, which lies to the right.

Christ Cross

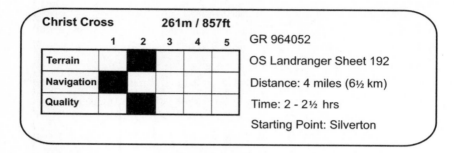

Christ Cross						261m / 857ft
	1	2	3	4	5	
Terrain		■				
Navigation	■					
Quality		■				

GR 964052

OS Landranger Sheet 192

Distance: 4 miles (6½ km)

Time: 2 - 2½ hrs

Starting Point: Silverton

This is the highest point of the range of red sandstone hills that lie around the Exe valley between Exeter and Tiverton. The hill is actually unnamed, the name Christ Cross relates to the road junction close to the summit. Neither is its summit pronounced in any way; it simply forms the highest point of the surrounding rolling farmland that drops westwards into the Exe valley.

The only practicable point to start a circular walk is the village of Silverton, which lies on the hill's southern slopes. The village is easily reached up a signposted lane from the A396 Exeter to Tiverton road. The car park is somewhat tucked away in a housing estate, although it is close on foot to the village centre. It can be found by turning northwards up Coach Lane from the easternmost of the two mini-roundabouts in the village. A subsequent left turn down Wyndham Road opposite the primary school then leads around and down to the car park (and toilets), which is located on the right.

From here, walk back up Wyndham Road, which is a dead end, to Coach Road at the school. A small footpath, between the school and houses, then runs up the right-hand side of the school and around its back to reach a stile into farmland. The right of way then crosses directly over the first small paddock to a stile and then continues straight ahead across the next, larger field, not following the left-hand margin, to a stile on the right-hand headland at the foot of the slope.

This stile gives access to a small back lane just below the hamlet of Livinghayes. A left turn leads towards the houses but, before they are reached, a right turn should be made almost immediately into a rising lane. This enters a field above and the path then continues along the left-hand margin before entering a green lane on the left and following that

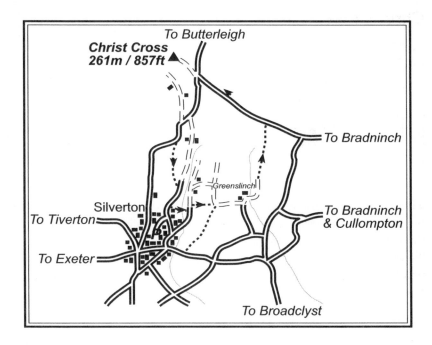

down to the next small hamlet of Greenslinch. There is little more than a farm here and our route skirts the majority of the buildings. Keeping straight across at the head of the public road, a track runs around the edge of the farm gardens to the buildings. Just before them, however, a track branches to the right and then proceeds to climb the slope, swinging back around to the left and eventually reaching, without deviation, the lane that runs along the top of the ridge between Christ Cross and Bradninch.

A section of roadwalking now follows along this enclosed lane to the left, which sets, after a small initial descent, a gently rising course to the road junction on the top of the hill. Here, the direct road rising up from Silverton on the left is met but our route crosses straight over onto the access track to the radio mast ahead on the summit. This track follows along the left-hand side of the first field before passing through a gate on the far side to the mast in the field beyond. However, the summit trig point lies in the hedge and can only be reached from the first field; it is completely hidden by hedge growth, 28 paces up from the track and just before the radio mast on the opposite side of the hedge.

The view is somewhat marred just here by the local hedges but, by walking to the radio mast, the view down the Exe valley to its estuary opens up beyond. The descent begins by returning to and following the main road down to Silverton. This starts to descend quite steeply and after a while passes a private road on the left and the entrance, on the right, to Land Farm, which is a small brewery. Still following the road, it shortly bends to the left and then after that back towards the right. On the second bend, where the road is slightly sunken, take off up the slope on the left to a double field gate and stile. The stile gives access to a narrow, enclosed path that follows the left-hand side of this first field, and the next, to reach a further lower lane. A right turn on this then leads back down to the primary school, from where a walk back through the estate leads to the car park.

Dundry Down

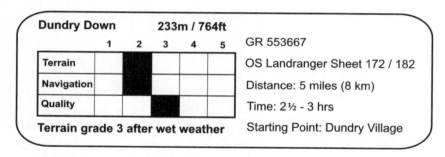

Dundry Down						GR 553667

	1	2	3	4	5
Terrain		■			
Navigation		■			
Quality			■		

233m / 764ft

Terrain grade 3 after wet weather

GR 553667

OS Landranger Sheet 172 / 182

Distance: 5 miles (8 km)

Time: 2½ - 3 hrs

Starting Point: Dundry Village

Dundry Down is a hill of contrasts. Underfoot, the wet, heavy soil gives rough fields of permanent grassland with tough, tedious and awkward walking. On the other hand, the views are quite superb and very photogenic, varying dramatically over the course of the walk. On the hill, a scrapyard stands in complete contrast to two quaint and tranquil villages, while the suburbs of Bristol encroach onto the hill's lower slopes in an endless array of tarmac and stone cladding. And, when you get to the end, don't hold your breath for the summit either.

The best place to begin is close to the summit in the small village of Dundry, which is easily reached from the Bristol to Chew Magna road that climbs up steep hairpins on the hill's northern slopes to cross the broad

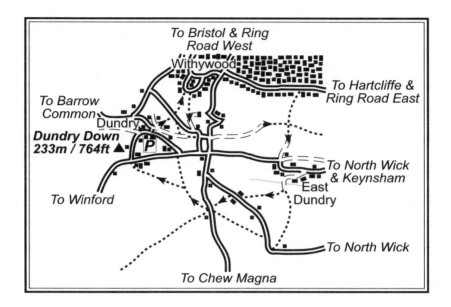

ridge. A small car park is signposted from the church along the Winford road and, as this is the only parking on the hill itself, it is prone to get quite busy. For those who wish to complete the full circuit, the first section of the walk involves a descent to the foot of the slopes. However, this could be easily avoided by walking along a lane below the church to reach the described route later on close to the main road over the ridge.

Begin by walking back to the road junction by the church and then turn left onto the Barrow Gurney road. In a matter of yards, this swings sharply left and a dead-end lane leads off to the right. Take this and almost immediately turn left into another but again quit this for a steep flight of steps on the right. Keep on straight down them to reach the lowest house of the village, beyond which fields lead down to the back of Bristol's suburbs. The field path begins almost opposite, down a narrow gap between a fence and a hedge that ends in a stile-like structure but with no crosspiece. The first field is damp underfoot and the path follows its right-hand margin to another stile in the bottom corner that again is lacking a crosspiece.

Over the stile, Oxleaze Lane is reached opposite a cottage at mid-height on the slopes. Just to the right of the cottage, the path continues into a rough, wet and seemingly unkempt field and descends to another stile-like structure at the bottom that is surrounded at times by yards of oozing mud on either side. The next field, a horse paddock, is not as rough but is just as wet and the path continues straight ahead into a thicket at the bottom through which it weaves its way. The route out to the highest suburban road lies down a narrow alley that appears to have been adopted by one of its neighbouring households as a dumping ground for garden waste.

Thus, the route reaches a backstreet of an area that is certainly not Bristol's most inviting suburb. Luckily though, our route turns to the right and then right again up the hill after about a hundred yards. The sunken lane, named Strawberry Lane, begins as a concrete trough whose walls have been decoratively painted. In wet weather, the lower reaches, which are undrained, turn into a large pond before the track starts to climb past the bottom of a flight of steps descending from a further residential road.

As the track turns uphill and leaves the estate behind, things start to improve and it turns into a rather pleasant, slightly sunken, green lane running between fields. At mid-height, it becomes surfaced as it joins the driveway of a cottage on the left; a further climb leads back up to Oxleaze Lane a little further along. From here, there is a good view back over Bristol and to the Clifton Suspension Bridge across the Avon and also the second Severn Bridge beyond. Turning along the road to the left, a row of cottages is passed, before the road finishes the ascent back to the ridge by turning to the right and splitting. Here, turn left and walk out onto the main road that crosses the ridge.

Opposite, a byway leads onwards along the slopes of Dundry Hill, passing a cottage on the right. It ends at a gateway into a field, where a farm track continues. However, just on the far side of the gate, where the cattle feeding station is positioned, the animals' cloven feet have churned up the wet soil into a massive quagmire that, certainly in wet weather, requires careful negotiation and possibly a little acrobatic work in very wet conditions! The right of way continues along the bottom of the field beyond to reach its far hedgerow, where another path is met that has climbed up the slope from Hartcliffe. Following this path to the right along the edge of this field and the next, a track is reached that leads past a radio mast to a farm at the top of the hamlet of East Dundry. Along this part of the route, a pleasant view opens up to the left of a section of the northern Mendip scarp.

To reach the road itself, it is first necessary to negotiate a heavy chain that has been slung across the roadway as a sort of seemingly unnecessary 'gate'. The road is met at a corner and it should be followed straight ahead, although it soon turns to the left and begins to descend into a deep valley that has eaten into the ridge. When a road junction is reached at Walnut Farm, turn sharply back to the right into a cul-de-sac that continues through the main part of the village, which is built of the local attractive honey-coloured stone. The last house is just above the beck itself and the track, now becoming rough, leads down to a ford. A couple of well-placed stones help with crossing the beck, on the other side of which the main lane should be left for a path that slants half right in the trees and crosses a stile.

This path then starts to climb straight up the very steep valley side to a hedgerow at the top. From here, the view back to the houses of East Dundry is as attractive as any classic view in the Cotswolds or Mendips and is certainly worthy of a photograph. The path now follows the right-hand margin of this field and then the next to reach a third behind the buildings of Watercress Farm. The route of the right of way across the final field is far from clear, although there is a gate half-right in the middle of the buildings. This leads onto the farm's driveway, which can then be followed out to a quiet lane opposite a tall and imposing red brick wall.

From here, our route takes us over to the southern side of the ridge and this is achieved by first walking along the road to the right until past the buildings. On the left, a gateway leads into a square, unused patch of land through which the drive runs to Upton Farm. Go through this gateway and cross the drive to reach a metal gate in the large field beyond. Although unmarked, this is a public footpath and it initially follows the left-hand edge of the field until that turns away to the left. This field is not as rough as the others and gives good walking conditions. Keep straight on where the fence swings left, to meet it again when it comes back again in due course. It can then be followed to another road that is reached over a stone stile just opposite a cottage. Immediately before the road is reached, the deep blue waters of the Chew Valley Lake appear on the left, beyond which the ground rises to the highest point of the Mendips, Beacon Batch.

Our route back towards the summit area makes use of further field paths that begin just to the right of the cottage over a stile on the far side of the road. Once in the field, turn to the right and follow the hedgerow into a second smaller field that often becomes a quagmire towards the far corner. Another stile gives access to the next small field, over which the path slants to reach a further radio mast. A tight squeeze then follows between the mast's perimeter fencing and a hedge on the left; a third stile gives access to a roadway over the fields.

Instead of following this roadway, however, cross the stile to its left. This stile leads into another large and rough grass field where a left turn is made to follow the fence and hedge along and into the next. At the far corner of that field, a collapsing gate, which is climbable with care and protected by a bramble thicket, gives access to the next field that drops to the left down towards the valley. However, keep along its top edge to a gate in the far corner, from where a trackway leads out to the Winford road out of Dundry village.

The summit is not far off now, although only ardent summiteers will bother to reach it. To do so, turn to the left along the road and, after a byway turns off to the left but before another on the right, an unmarked and easily missed stone stile gives access into the undulating field on the right that lies at the back of the scrapyard. This field contains various seemingly artificial pits and mounds, with the trig point standing atop the highest of these, although doubts must be raised as to whether it does actually qualify as the true summit. Otherwise, you can take your pick of any other part of the surrounding fields to be the top.

Although in theory the right of way leads on and through the scrapyard, you may prefer to be tactful and avoid upsetting the large and vicious-looking guard dogs by backtracking to the previous junction where the route first met the Winford Road. Opposite, a road, signposted to Dundry, leads along past the entrance to the scrapyard and back to the car park. As for an alternative summit, any point along this road would do and certainly be much less hassle. Thus, the mixed route is brought to an end, on the top of the northern scarp, from where the city of Bristol is laid out as a toy town at your feet.

Section 3 – The Wessex Downs and the Isle of Wight

The Solent from Portsmouth and Southampton Water to the Itchen. That river to its source at Preston Candover. The B3046 from there to Basingstoke and the River Loddon from there to the Thames at Shiplake. The River Thames to Abingdon, the Vale of the White Horse to Swindon and the clay vale to Malmesbury. The River Avon to Bradford-on-Avon and River Frome to Frome. The Taunton railway to the Somerset Levels and their eastern margin to the Parrett, which is followed to its source. Directly overland to the River Axe and then the Axe Valley to Seaton. Coast from there around the south of the Isle of Wight to Portsmouth.

NAME	HEIGHT	IN SECTION	IN ENGLAND	IN BRITAIN
Walbury Hill	297m / 974ft	01 of 09	138 of 184	1375 of 1552
Long Knoll	288m / 945ft	02 of 09	144 of 184	1394 of 1552
Lewesdon Hill	279m / 915ft	03 of 09	146 of 184	1413J of 1552
Win Green	277m / 910ft	04 of 09	148 of 184	1418J of 1552
St Boniface Down	240m / 786ft	05 of 09	166 of 184	1476 of 1552
Brighstone Down	214m / 701ft	06 of 09	175 of 184	1503 of 1552
Swyre Head	208m / 682ft	07 of 09	176 of 184	1506 of 1552
Hardown Hill	207m / 678ft	08 of 09	177 of 184	1508J of 1552
Nine Barrow Down	199m / 653ft	09 of 09	179 of 184	1518 of 1552

The Wessex Downs is the largest area of chalk downland in southern England. This is a landscape of rolling tablelands, whale-backed ridges and gracefully curving escarpments. The downland is broken into a number of ridge systems that radiate out from Salisbury Plain to all points of the

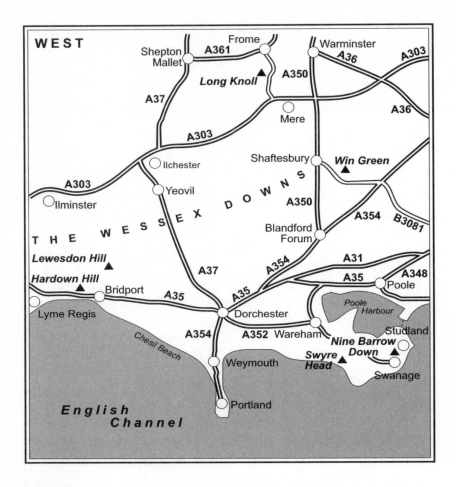

compass and extend northwards all the way through Lincolnshire and into Yorkshire (Volumes 2 and 3). Here, though, the landscape's boundless wide horizons are interrupted only by dry, hidden valleys and the stupendous cliffs of the Channel coast.

Wessex was the homeland of the West Saxons and has no specific defined boundaries. This section, in truth, does contain areas that are not chalk and the summit of Swyre Head is in fact constructed from Portland and Purbeck limestones that have been exposed on the surface as a result of Alpine crumpling, which has added so much diversity to places such as Purbeck and the Isle of Wight.

The best period in which to begin a geological explanation is the

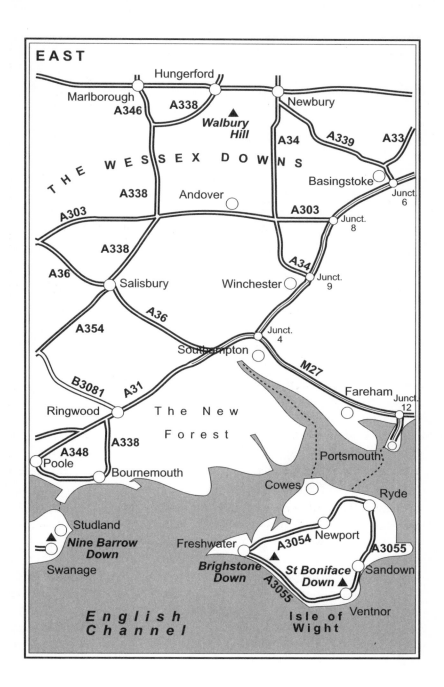

Jurassic period, in which the Portland limestones were deposited. During this time, much of Britain was invaded by a shallow sea that was rich in marine life. The lowest section of the Jurassic marine deposits are known as the Lias and these consist of a cyclical sequence of limestones and shales that are prominently exposed in Dorset's sea cliffs. Later in the sequence, the ocean began to retreat southwards, depositing the oolitic limestones of the Cotswolds (Section 5) and the yellow Bath Stone, before depositing the youngest of the Jurassic limestones – the Portland Stone. This bright white limestone is very much prized for building work due to its ease of working and even, grainy texture and it has been widely used in many famous London buildings, including the Houses of Parliament.

In amongst these layers were clays, most prominent in this area being the latest additions – the Oxford and Kimmeridge Clays; Jurassic clays are responsible for much of the coastal slippage around Lyme Regis. The Jurassic sequence is, however, discussed in more detail in Section 5, where it is a more prominent feature in the landscape.

There was no permanent deposition of rocks in this area during the Lower Cretaceous period. However, when the landscape subsided in the middle of the Cretaceous, the sea re-entered and began to deposit marine beds that were cemented together to form the Lower Greensand rock. As the sea deepened further, the sediments changed from sandstones to clays – the Gault Clay – and then back to a less resistant sandstone – the Upper Greensand. The Greensand beds and the Gault Clay are to be found in the Wessex landscape and are responsible for much of the coastal slippage in areas such as the Isle of Wight. They are, however, much more prominent in the landscape of the Weald (Section 4).

Further subsidence of the land surface allowed this sea to deepen and spread over the whole of Britain. This shallow clear sea was home to a large population of small scaly creatures called coccolithophores – a tiny plankton. Their corpses collected on the sea floor and their scales, coccoliths, compacted to form a very pure limestone sequence – this is the chalk itself. Although generally soft and very porous, unlike the Carboniferous Mountain Limestones of the Mendips (Section 2), for example, the chalk does contain a total of three harder beds in amongst the soft sheets of calcium carbonate. At the same time, sponges were also living in the ocean and their skeletons formed a glass-like stone called flints. As erosive forces slowly began to eat away at the chalk, the flints were left behind on the surface to become mixed with the later Tertiary deposits.

By now, nearly all the rocks of the Wessex hills had been deposited, although various massive tectonic upheavals were to shape the landscape into that seen today. Firstly, the Atlantic ocean was about to form and this was preceded by a doming of western Britain, causing a north-west to south-east dip and forcing the retreat of the shallow chalk-depositing sea that was covering Britain. The chalk was then eroded from much of the resulting highlands of western and northern Britain, being confined only to the southern and eastern fringes of England.

The same period also saw Africa collide into southern Europe, crumpling the crust and building the massive mountains of the Alps. This orogeny, or mountain building episode, was not, however, confined to the Alps. The crust of southern England was also crushed and crumpled to produce a network of anticlines and synclines, of which the Weald (Section 4) is one of the largest examples. This crumpling also formed the contorted vertical and horizontal strata in Lulworth Cove.

In Wessex, there is a coastal anticline, the axis of which runs through the Isle of Wight and then through Purbeck and Portland, although parts of this have now been eaten away by the waves of the English Channel. A large syncline, known as the Hampshire Basin, also developed around Southampton, the New Forest, Poole and to the north of the Isle of Wight, although large sections of this are now flooded by the sea. Finally, another syncline developed to the east of Newbury through Reading and around London; this is known as the London Basin. In both these low-lying areas, Tertiary deposits of both marine and fresh water beds are to be found as the crust rose and then subsided as a result of the continued mountain building.

Any such deposits have been worn away off the top of the chalk downland, leaving behind only large cemented blocks of sand and gravel, known as sarsens, which were used in the construction of many of Wessex's ancient archaeological remains, such as the stone circles of Avebury and the long barrows at West Kennett near Avebury and Wayland's Smithy near Uffington. However, a clay capping does remain in many places where, mixed with flints from the Cretaceous erosion, it forms damp and heavy soils that are in complete contrast to the light, dry and free-draining soils of the chalklands. The flints that remained in the uneroded chalk then consolidated into certain layers within the rock strata.

Despite being a soft rock, the chalk was spared from the erosion by its covering of Tertiary rocks. This capping was not broken until the tundra conditions that prevailed around the Ice Age. Although the ice sheets never reached this far south, the climate was severely cold and this allowed water to collect in cracks in the rock during the day and freeze at night. As water freezes, it expands, progressively widening the cracks until the rock shatters; this is how the Tertiary crust disintegrated into sarsens.

Chalk is a very porous rock and this allows it to soak up rainwater like a giant sponge, holding it in aquifers and pores in the rock. This effect makes the downlands very dry, with springs emerging lower in the summer and somewhat higher in winter forming seasonal streams called winterbournes. However, at the time of the Ice Age, the chalk 'sponge' became frozen solid, which enabled rainwater to carve valleys into its plateau-like surface that today are dry for much of their length with some supporting winterbournes in their middle and lower reaches. The ability of chalk to soak up rainwater is the main reason why such a soft rock has been largely able to escape water erosion and form such an elevated upland.

The ridge system has also developed from the Alpine crumpling, although in a peculiarly inverse way. The crumples formed original ridges, which were much more prone to erosion than the surrounding chalk tablelands. Their tops were eroded away, exposing the greensand and clays below, upon which the erosive forces quickly worked wearing these areas into low vales, such as the Vale of Pewsey, that are bounded by steep scarps and chalk ridges. These chalk ridges, although higher than the surrounding chalk plateaux, are *not* the ridges that formed directly from the Alpine folding, but rather the lower slopes of those original ridges that have had their tops 'cut off'.

The same happened with the anticline that stretched through the Isle of Wight and Purbeck. On the Isle of Wight, a central Greensand and Gault Clay vale developed between two chalk ridges and these ridges and valleys stretched unbroken into Purbeck. The only difference in Purbeck was that the southern ridge was broader and therefore higher. This has meant that erosion here has exposed the late Jurassic Portland limestone on Swyre Head and the Kimmeridge Clay of similar age at its scarp foot before the sea cliffs.

Behind this anticlinal structure, a large river system existed, known as the Solent River, which rose in Devon and flowed eastwards through what is now the Solent. Rivers that rose on the original Isle of Wight–Purbeck anticline flowed northwards to join the Solent River and, even once the central clay vale had formed, they maintained their courses, cutting deep gashes in the northern chalk ridge, such as at Corfe Castle on Purbeck and Blackwater on the Isle of Wight.

After the formation of the Channel (see Section 4), the sea constantly ate away at the chalk until it broke through and flooded large areas of the Hampshire Basin, leaving the Isle of Wight as an island. Today, it is still eating away at the chalk and Purbeck limestone in other places. At Lulworth Cove, it breached the natural barrier and excavated a large bay in the clay behind. At places such as Lyme Regis and on the south coast of the Isle of Wight, where clays form the cliffs, the unstable wet clay has slumped seawards, sending material from the upper strata crashing into the sea, taking roads and buildings with it, to form an interesting undercliff of tumbled blocks and landslips.

Thus, the landscape becomes recognisable as that seen today. Around Lyme Regis, the chalk meets the sea before running further inland over Lewesdon Hill. Coastal summits, such as the heather-clad Hardown Hill and the bracken-clad Golden Cap, are formed from the greensand. Within the central chalklands, high summits, such as Walbury Hill and Win Green, stand overlooking steep scarps and gentle dipslopes, while Purbeck and the Isle of Wight present a contorted and beautiful landscape of Alpine crumples and folds.

Accommodation

In tourist areas, such as the Isle of Wight, Purbeck and the Dorset coast, there is plenty of accommodation, although if you wish to stay outside the seaside resorts then it is certainly advisable to book in advance, especially in the summer season. Further north and east, accommodation becomes increasingly sparse, although, again, popular tourist areas such as Winchester and Salisbury are quite well served. Problems may occur in the far north-east of the section, in places such as Newbury, where accommodation tends to become more limited outside the hotels and pubs in the towns themselves. There are youth hostels at Streatley-on-

Thames, The Ridgeway (near Wantage), Winchester, Portsmouth, Totland Bay and Sandown (the Isle of Wight), Burley (the New Forest), Salisbury, Lulworth and Swanage (Purbeck), Portland, Litton Cheney (near Dorchester) and Beer (near Seaton).

Walbury Hill

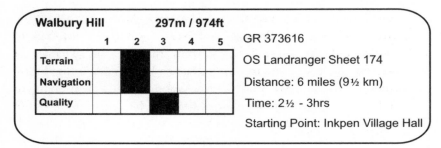

Walbury Hill						297m / 974ft
	1	2	3	4	5	GR 373616
Terrain		■				OS Landranger Sheet 174
Navigation		■				Distance: 6 miles (9½ km)
Quality			■			Time: 2½ - 3hrs
						Starting Point: Inkpen Village Hall

This is a very varied walk on high chalk downland visiting both Combe Gibbet Long Barrow as well as the hill fort on Walbury Hill. Although it is quite possible to drive by public road virtually to the summit, the best starting point for a circular walk starting from valley level is Inkpen Village. Many of the public footpaths on which this route runs are far from distinct on the ground and those in the valley can be very soggy after rain.

Inkpen Village Hall is just to the south of the Old Post Office (marked on the OS Landranger map), next to the playing field. If the car park is locked or full, it is possible to park nearby on the road. Begin by walking north up the road from the car park for a few yards before turning right down a tarmacked road. Shortly, this turns into a gravel track, goes through a gate and turns right. Once the corner is turned, a path through a steel gate on the left (marked by a rusted fingerpost on the right) runs down and across the lawn of the large house to a stile giving access to an agricultural field. Go straight across this field, aiming just to the right of the farm buildings, to a gate giving access to the road. Turn left on the road (straight on, on the ground) for about ten yards until the road bears left, where the route continues straight on through the gate ahead. Follow

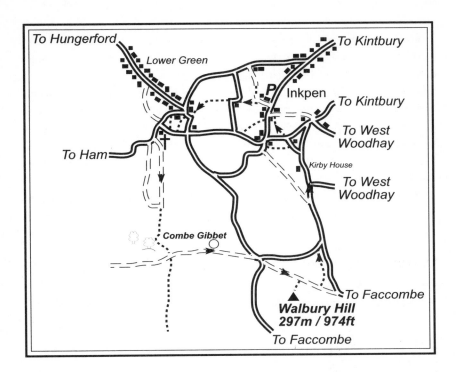

the edge of the enclosure round to the left and through another gate giving access to a narrow enclosed track running to the right.

This path eventually bears left and, after passing through a thicket, comes out into a patch of more open land. Follow the hedge to the right and then to the left, soon going down a leafy avenue to the right between houses that runs out on to another road near a junction. Turn left and follow the road signposted 'Ham and Shalbourne'. Follow the road past a turn to the left signposted to Inkpen Church and then turn left down a track. Follow this track, which soon bears right and up the edge of the field. When it bears right again, keep straight on up a footpath running up a leafy tree-lined green lane which eventually gives access to the open hill.

Start by going straight up the slope and then turn left following a distinct, steeply rising trod. This finishes on the narrow chalk ridge. Turn left and eventually right through a gate near Combe Gibbet that gives access to the track on the right. Pass the gibbet and long barrow and follow the track down to the road. Go straight on and follow the sunken roadway that runs up into the hill fort with its earthen ramparts guarding a large central enclosure. About halfway through the fort turn right on another track which, after 100 yards, leads to the trig point, the top of which is just visible from the main track through the fort. Retrace your steps to the main track and turn right following it out of the fort. Once out of the fort do not turn immediately left, but keep straight on for about 100 yards until turning left over a stile (signposted). Bear half left past another stile but with no fence and follow the path down through a small wood to meet the road.

Turn left down the road ignoring a road immediately on the left and then one on the right. Continue past Kirby House ignoring a road on the right and instead continue up a small hill and on to a T-junction. Here, follow a footpath opposite, straight across a horse paddock and over another stile. Follow the path now on the right-hand side of the hedge and over yet another stile. When an unmade road is met, turn left and after a few yards this reaches the main road in Inkpen. A right turn leads shortly back to the Village Hall car park.

Long Knoll

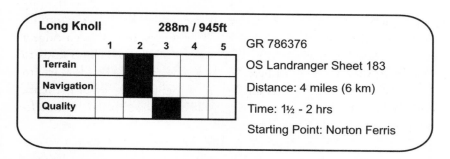

Long Knoll						288m / 945ft
	1	2	3	4	5	
Terrain		■				
Navigation		■				
Quality			■			

GR 786376

OS Landranger Sheet 183

Distance: 4 miles (6 km)

Time: 1½ - 2 hrs

Starting Point: Norton Ferris

Norton Ferris, the starting point for this route, is a small hamlet on the Mere to Frome road, which is easily missed. There is parking at the entrance to a little used byway on the left and a massive bus stop but other than that opportunities are limited. Long Knoll stands alone and is a sharp ridge that towers above the surrounding landscape. It is quite unlike the other hills of the region and stands out to all who pass by it.

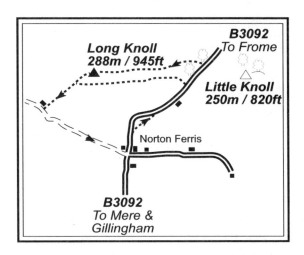

Leave Norton Ferris by walking north on the B3092. Shortly, a Wiltshire County Council footpath sign stands alone on the right-hand verge pointing out a right of way clearly blocked by barbed wire. This path does cut a corner off and avoids some roadwalking, so, with care, cross the barbed wire and walk across the field, passing the corner of the wood, to emerge once more back on the road through an unblocked but unsignposted gap in the hedge just short of the buildings of Knoll Farm. Continue up the road as it tucks itself under the steep slopes of Long Knoll; ignore the first signposted footpath on the left but take the second. This runs back on itself through a wood to emerge on the steep ridge a considerable distance above the road. A steep one-in-one climb leads to the eastern summit. Beyond here, the path descends a short distance, to the left of the wood, before changing to the right-hand side of the fence and ascending to the summit and trig point which are situated on the left-hand side of the fence, reached through a gap.

Descend onwards on the left-hand side of the fence to reach a stile at the bottom of the very steep hill. The path continues on through fields to reach the farm buildings at Homestalls. Pass through the farmyard and turn left on the byway at the front. Continue straight on before soon taking a track on the left, which then bends back to the right and leads directly back to Norton Ferris.

Lewesdon Hill

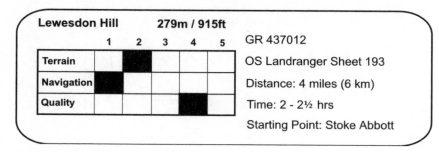

Lewesdon Hill	279m / 915ft				
	1	2	3	4	5
Terrain		■			
Navigation	■				
Quality				■	

GR 437012

OS Landranger Sheet 193

Distance: 4 miles (6 km)

Time: 2 - 2½ hrs

Starting Point: Stoke Abbott

Lewesdon Hill is the highest summit in Dorset, although it only overtops its nearby neighbour Pilsdon Pen by a few feet. It sits at the apex of the most northerly of the two ridges near Lyme Regis and supports a varied view southwards to the sea and northwards over lower ground well into Somerset. The best place to start a circular walk is the small village of Stoke Abbott, which nestles below the chalk ridge.

There is parking in the village along the Beaminster road near to its junction with the Broadwindsor road. Here there is a small spring and, where the road is wide, there is parking on the west side up to a sharp right bend. Around this, there is the New Inn, which has its own sizeable car park for patrons.

The route starts off by following the Beaminster road past the New Inn. Fairly soon, a footpath turns off to the left but our route follows the next road to the left, which is also a bridleway. This private drive passes a house on the right and then enters an overhung, sunken, tree-lined lane. This deep and dark place is refreshingly cool on hot summer days and the roadway winds through it for some time as it climbs up the slope. When it emerges, it bends to the right and then continues up the slope.

Soon, a permitted path is to be found climbing up the left bank and then running above but parallel to the roadway until it ends at a house on the ridge itself. On this part of the route, notice the strip lynchets in the field up to the left. The path enters the top of the house's gardens through a gate and then leaves through the left-hand one of the two ahead; a junction of paths is then reached.

Here, the Wessex Ridgeway is joined and this track should then be followed along to the left, along a fenced lane at the top of this steeply sloping field and then along the bottom of the next few. All the time, the

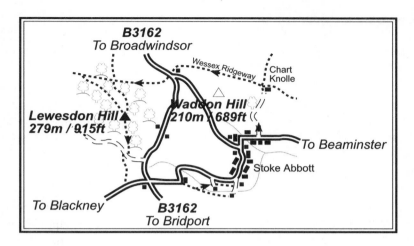

track is becoming more pronounced and after a while it curves to the left and passes through a farmyard to reach the road, once more back on the ridge crest. Straight across, a trackway (still the Wessex Ridgeway) leads onwards and now more steeply uphill. In due course it comes under the tree-covered upper slopes of the hill but it stays close to the bottom of the wood as it enters the National Trust-owned land. When the hedge disappears on the right, the northwards view appears for the first and last time.

The track now becomes increasingly wet, necessitating, in most conditions, an escape up onto a path running along the left-hand bank. Just beyond this, though, a path is met climbing up the hill from the right and this should be followed to the left. The final climb is now ahead and the path continues under the beech trees, climbing back leftwards across the scarp to reach more open ground on the summit area. The summit now lies ahead at the very furthest end of the flat table-like summit plateau. In summer, the view is somewhat restricted by the tree-growth but a fine southwards view over Hardown Hill and Golden Cap to the sea is visible through the branches of a tall pine.

The route of descent now lies down the steep south ridge that drops immediately from the summit. The path is now clear until the ridge levels off a bit where there may be some uncertainty. However, the route keeps on directly ahead and down a wide track on the far side before once more dropping steeply to meet a metalled farm roadway through a gate, where there is limited parking. To the left, this lane leads out onto the Bridport to Broadwindsor road high above Stoke Abbott.

The village lies in the valley ahead and is best reached by following this road to the right to reach a crossroads. Here, a left turn leads down the hill and before too long a farm is reached. Since the crossroads, we have been following the Jubilee Trail and this is now followed all the way back to Stoke Abbott. To begin with, it leads down the right-hand side of the house ahead and then out over a stile into the large sloping field beyond. Initially, it follows the right-hand edge but soon, at a waymarker, the trail turns sharply to the left and drops down to cross the small stream in the bottom of the valley. Although there is a footbridge, a quagmire must be crossed first to reach it.

Another steeply sloping field is then entered where the path slants left up the bank and then across a stile into the driveway of the tranquil house that lies down to the right. Straight across, another stile leads into a further field and over that into another where the path slants half right; this then reaches a small lane on the edge of the village. A left turn leads out past a house onto the public road and this contours along above the church and through the village to the starting point.

Win Green

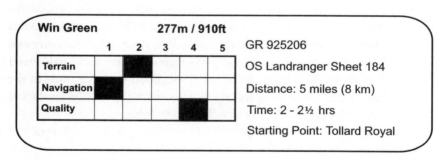

Win Green		277m / 910ft			
	1	2	3	4	5
Terrain		■			
Navigation	■				
Quality				■	

GR 925206

OS Landranger Sheet 184

Distance: 5 miles (8 km)

Time: 2 - 2½ hrs

Starting Point: Tollard Royal

The northern slopes of Win Green fall steeply away to Ludwell and the A30 but the southern aspect is much more interesting. Here, the dipslope is carved into deep and interesting hidden valleys, which contain many secrets. Although there is a car park close to the summit, the best approach is up Ashcombe Bottom from Tollard Royal.

Tollard Royal lies on the Shaftesbury to Ringwood road and there is some

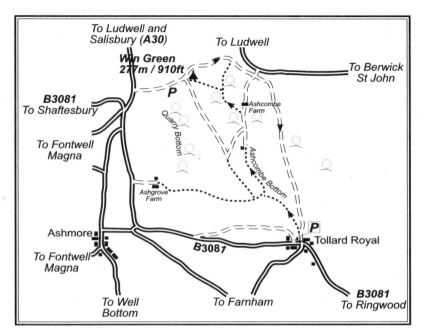

car parking around the village green and pond, although options are limited. Leave the village by the track next to the duck pond, keeping straight on at the first fork, opposite a farm entrance. This track, the Wessex Ridgeway, soon becomes grassy underfoot as it passes through the fields behind the village. Before long, it passes through a rusty gate and then descends down into the valley bottom for the first time where the valley splits. Pass over two stiles on the right and then bear sharp right up the floor of the right-hand valley. A chalk track, slightly to the left throughout, soon descends to the valley floor and this should be followed past a charming cottage on the left before it turns sharply left with the valley below Ashcombe Farm.

Continuing up the valley, the track shortly forks; take the left fork and then the next left fork. This leads to the mouth of a side valley on the left and then up steeply into the woods on the far side. Here the main track should be followed which turns sharply left up through the woods on the ridge to emerge onto the open hillside. The path runs up to the top of this field, turning left and running along the headland to a gate. However, instead of passing through the gate, climb a stile on the right and then bear back to the trig point and viewfinder, which are now clearly to be seen in front of a large clump of trees.

From the summit, follow a grassy path to the right of the trees and then down the main ridge to the right around the head of the valley. At a sharp col, it meets a byway that then runs around the northern slopes of a small hill. When at the next col, a path on the right runs back down into Ashcombe Bottom to rejoin the outward route. This may be taken in preference to the circuit described here, which follows the dusty byway back to Tollard Royal. If the byway option is chosen, continue on the track, meeting another road on the top of Monk's Down, at which point the signposted byway swings around to the right and descends gradually at first, then finally steeply, back to the pond at Tollard Royal.

St Boniface Down

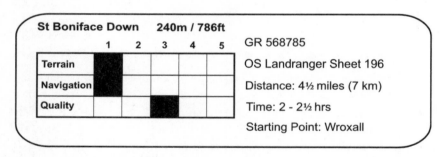

St Boniface Down	240m / 786ft				
	1	2	3	4	5
Terrain	■				
Navigation	■				
Quality			■		

GR 568785

OS Landranger Sheet 196

Distance: 4½ miles (7 km)

Time: 2 - 2½ hrs

Starting Point: Wroxall

The name of the highest summit on the Isle of Wight is a matter of debate. The downland ridge to the west is called Littleton Down, the downland ridge to the east is called Bonchurch Down and the south-western ridge is called St Boniface Down; all ridges seem to have equal claim to the apparently nameless summit where they meet. However, certainly in hillwalking terms, St Boniface Down appears to be the most commonly accepted name, so that is the one used here. On the hill's southern slopes, the ground drops steeply to the towns of Bonchurch, Cowlease and Ventnor, which all merge into one along the slumping shoreline. So urban is the setting that from a walking point of view, the only sensible route of ascent is from the north and the large village of Wroxall appears to be the best starting point.

In the village, the free car park is signposted up a side road that runs east

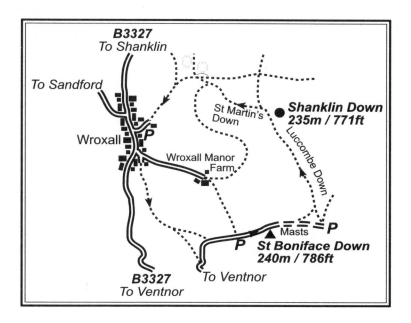

from the main road opposite The Worsley pub. To start with, the road should be followed back out to the main street and a left turn should be made to descend to the village store in the bottom of the valley. Here, the road starts to climb and should be left where it bends to the right for a small lane just to the left of the Four Seasons Inn. In turn, this road should be left for a smaller one on the right that leads into a small estate and, where that bends sharply to the right, a green lane should be followed ahead.

With Wroxall now behind, the lane climbs with no deviation through the farmland on the lower slopes to arrive on the largely uncultivated downland that forms the summit of the hill. Following the hedge on the left, the path swings left and joins with another before entering one final field. Still stay on the left and follow the path up along its edge to reach the ridge over a stile at the top of the field.

The sea is not yet in view but, climbing ahead around the left of some gorse bushes, it soon appears around to the right. Here, the path splits and, instead of taking a narrower path through the dwarf gorse on the right, keep to the left on a grassy track that runs parallel to it. This continues on and runs parallel to the road that has climbed up from Ventnor to the ridge. The summit is clear in the view ahead, being adorned by radio masts and raised bunkers. The complex here was the testing station for the new radar technology when it was being developed during the Second World War and thus has a great deal of wartime history surrounding it.

Just before the perimeter fence is reached, at the third car parking area on the road to the right, the best seawards view can be obtained from the National Trust information board. Now follow the road onwards and, shortly, this reaches its highest point on a left-hand bend. With the exception of man-made mounds and other monstrosities, ardent summiteers will no doubt wish to point out that the natural ground level is perhaps at most one or two feet higher inside the perimeter fence but, for most people, that makes little difference.

The descent back to Wroxall takes a circuitous route over Luccombe and Shanklin Downs, before dropping off down the hill to the village. Thus, follow the road onwards to its end and then continue down a rough track that swings to the right. Here, leave it for a path on the left that runs through a kissing gate and contours around the head of a shallow valley to reach the track on the heather and dwarf gorse-clad ridge of Luccombe Down. Following this to the left, the route passes through an area of thicker gorse before running parallel to the margin of a field on the right. A stile in the hedge soon gives access to this and the domed summit of Shanklin Down with its highly elevated trig point can be reached by slanting half right and slightly uphill. From here, the sands of Shanklin and Sandown gently curve around the bay and past the pier, before the island's southern chain of downland culminates in the dazzling white expanse of Culver Cliff.

Turning your back on that view, walk westwards to another stile in the hedge that once more gives access to the track running along the down. This should now be followed to the right to enter another field, where the main path slants off half left, across St Martin's Down, beginning the descent back to Wroxall. Just before the field's far hedge is reached, fork right and enter a lower field, where the path descends around the edge of a massive chalk pit, before making a beeline for a prominent wooden gate at the bottom of the field. Do not use this, however, instead continue along the base of the field until a stile on the right gives access to the wood and a path running along just inside it.

Follow this to the left and out over a stile into a further small field just above Wroxall. The path follows around the right-hand side and then the bottom margin of this field to reach, after a stile on the right, the point where the Wroxall path leaves the field in the bottom left corner. After passing through a small copse, the path crosses a stile and enters a narrow lane enclosed by a fence on the left and a wooded hedge on the right; this path should now be followed to the end of a road at the edge of Wroxall. The village centre does not now lie far ahead and is best reached by continuing ahead down this lane. In fact, this road, after widening somewhat, leads directly back to the car park and starting point.

Brighstone Down

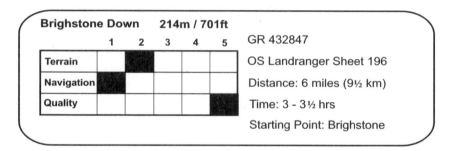

Brighstone Down	214m / 701ft					
	1	2	3	4	5	GR 432847
Terrain		■				OS Landranger Sheet 196
Navigation	■					Distance: 6 miles (9½ km)
Quality					■	Time: 3 - 3½ hrs
						Starting Point: Brighstone

Brighstone Down is the highest point on the northern chain of downland on the Isle of Wight, which culminates spectacularly in the west in the cliff face of Tennyson Down and the chalk sea stacks of the Needles. The best place to begin an ascent is the small village of Brighstone, from which the Down takes its name. This small and rather quaint village nestles below the hill's slopes along the island's southern shore between Blackgang and Freshwater.

The car park and toilets are in the village between the church and post office, off the main street down a small signposted lane. To begin the walk, return to the main road and make a left and then a right turn. This leads up a small lane past the post office, National Trust gift shop and an interesting museum charting the village's history. This road soon comes to an end at a T-junction but a rough track opposite, signposted to the Downs, begins the ascent up a deep sunken lane, faced in places with vertical sandstone

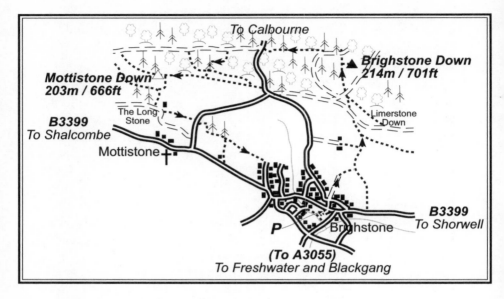

exposures. Above this, it reaches the first scarp slope and turns to the right, climbing across the slope and gaining height quickly. Ignoring a path to the left at mid-height, continue to the top of this scarp and follow the path onwards to meet another climbing from the right in front of a fence.

Here, turn left and follow this broad track ahead as it winds across a slight valley to reach the foot of the chalk scarp of Limerstone Down. Although the slope is very steep, the path slants across the face to the left, easing the gradient of the ascent; a crosstracks is reached at the top of this hill. Ahead lies the edge of a large area of scrubby woodland and a path opposite leads into it. This shortly joins with another and, after ignoring a track to the right and crossing over a first crosstracks, a second is reached. Here, the Tennyson Trail, which runs from the Needles to near Newport, is crossed. Following our track onwards, the woodland gives way to gorse heath as the track, now broad and grassy, climbs the final slopes until a grassy path on the right cuts through the gorse to the elevated trig point.

From here, the views are slightly restricted by the stand of woodland to the north and indeed the coastal panorama is not quite as good as it was from the top of the first scarp. However, the best viewpoint, the top of Mottistone Down, is yet to be reached.

That is the next destination and it is reached by returning to the grassy track and turning to the right, into the more substantial woodland to the north. Not far inside it, a junction of woodland tracks is reached and here a left turn should be made. This track soon starts to bend to the left and it should be left for a path that initially slants half right but soon rejoins the original line, following it in a dead-straight beeline for some considerable distance through the dappled shade of the trees before, after a few final bends on the lower slopes, meeting the Brighstone to Calbourne road in the woodland hollow of Calbourne Bottom.

Opposite and just slightly to the right, the path continues into the trees, now as a broad forest road. Although a path initially turns to the left by a yellow-banded waymarker, continue along the track for some time until, by a second such marker, another path slants off to the left. This now proceeds to climb out of the small valley up some steep steps, not far above which lies a bench. From here, the yellow-topped waymarkers continue up the slope and then along it for some distance before climbing once again to meet a higher forest trackway. Crossing this straight over, the now yellow- and blue-banded waymarkers lead onwards over another woodland path to emerge onto the gently rising grassy ridge of Mottistone Down. From here, the coastal panorama is superb to the east, although the westwards view cannot be appreciated until the summit is reached. Therefore, turn to the right and climb gently on the flint track, or on the springy turf on either side, to reach a gate, just through which is the summit, marked by a handful of ancient tumuli. From here, the sheer chalk cliff on Tennyson Down, further along the coast, clearly steals the scene, although, unfortunately, the Needles themselves remain out of sight, tucked away slightly around the corner.

The return down the hill to Brighstone will not disappoint either, as the route is still full of interest. Return to the gate and descend following the fence on the summit side to the bottom of the slope, where a path runs back right to reach a bridleway at a gate. Turning down through this, the bridleway continues down inside the edge of the wood to reach a gate at the bottom and the end of the bridleway. Through the gate, a left turn on the gravelled track leads down to an ancient standing stone, known as the Long Stone, just above a warm red-brick house of the same name.

Keeping straight ahead, the path leaves the track, which now turns to the right and crosses the field ahead, before cutting out to the charmingly named Strawberry Lane down a narrow green lane. On Strawberry Lane, a right turn soon leads to a signposted track on the left that curves through a field to a gate at its top to give access to Grammar's Common. On the common, the right of way turns to the right down a broad track that contours around the small hill through the tall Scots pines. In due course, the track starts to drop to a crosspaths but keep straight on and follow the track ahead and then around to the right to reach the edge of the common.

Here, a path continues down the descending ridge before cutting through the outlying houses of Brighstone to reach a small back lane, which, to the right, leads out to a bend on the Brighstone to Mottistone road. Now following this road to the left (actually ahead on the ground), it turns to the left and then, after two roads on the right, a signposted path takes off down an alley on the right. This eventually reaches a small estate road that should be followed to the left. To reach the village centre and car park, take the second road on the left, which soon crosses a small stream on a bridge. A path follows on the far bank to the right and, after crossing a further road and passing the end of another, it ends on a third opposite the sports pitch and playground on the other bank. Just slightly to the right, the path continues on the other side of the road to the car park, which is entered near the toilet block.

Swyre Head

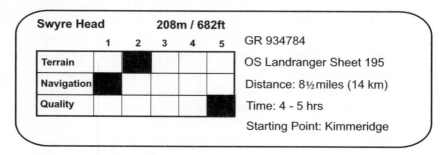

Swyre Head			208m / 682ft		
	1	2	3	4	5
Terrain		■			
Navigation	■				
Quality					■

GR 934784

OS Landranger Sheet 195

Distance: 8½ miles (14 km)

Time: 4 - 5 hrs

Starting Point: Kimmeridge

Swyre Head is the highest of Purbeck's hills and lies on the western end of the peninsula, where it merges into the Dorset downland, not far from the village of Lulworth and its famous cove. Despite the large number of warning notices about the Lulworth military range, this walk stays well outside it and thus is open all the year round.

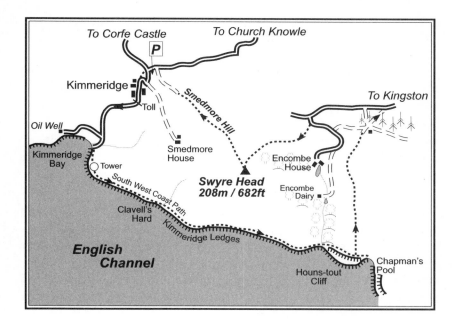

The hill itself is part of the southern of Purbeck's two downland ridges and stands back from the cliff edge by about half a mile, atop the point where two graceful curves on the ridge's southern scarp slope meet. The best place to begin the walk is the small village of Kimmeridge where there are two parking areas – one on the ridge and one on the shore in the bay. Since the road to the shore is a toll road operated by the Smedmore Estate, there seems little point in parking there when there is free parking in a quarry on the left where the dead-end road into the village starts to descend after crossing the ridge.

From the old quarry, walk out to the road and turn to the right up to the road junction on the ridge crest. Here, turn sharp left on a path over a stile that drops down through a field to rejoin the road by the church in Kimmeridge, cutting off a large corner. Walk down the road through the village and then on down the toll road (which is free for pedestrians as it is a public footpath). This leads around a small hill and down towards the shore at the left-hand side of the broad bay. Over to the other side, an oil installation pumping oil trapped in the Jurassic strata appears prominently in the view. Towards the foot of the slope, ignore a road on the right that leads to the main car park. Instead, keep straight ahead but soon turn to the right into another car park with signposted toilets and then leave that down a footpath at its lower end that is signposted to the quay.

This crosses a babbling brook, which discharges into the bay, to reach the slipway, marine reserve centre and toilets. Our route keeps left, parallel to the quay, to a flight of steps. These are part of the South West Coast Path and they lead steeply up to the ruins of Clavel Tower on the top of this first headland. From here, take the time to look westwards along the cliffs and headlands towards Lulworth. This view becomes ever more captivating with height and distance, with Swyre Head itself being the best viewpoint.

Our route now follows the undulating Coast Path along the clifftop. After three downs and two ups, the path reaches the first wide bay of Clavell's Hard, although this is still guarded by cliffs. A few small streams are crossed on wooden footbridges, before the path climbs up to Rope Lake Head. Those interested in coastal erosion will note the successive wave-cut platforms of the Kimmeridge Ledges that stretch outwards from the cliff toe on the right, marking the continuing erosion of the cliff. Beyond this next headland, where the coast curves slightly left, the path descends before climbing over a smaller bump to reach Eldon Seat below Swyre Head up on the left.

However, the Coast Path is set to descend yet again across the mouth of the valley of Encombe. By now, you will have realised why the Coast Path walkers that are passing you look so tired and weary, muttering something about a few hundred steps here and another few hundred there. However, looking ahead, the headland of Houns-tout Cliff rears skywards and that is our next destination. First, though, the path crosses the valley stream, which, diverted from its natural course to prevent further erosion of its valley, creates a small waterfall where it cascades over a small cliff to the beach. The climb then begins, only slackening off for a short section in the middle. Looking on the bright side though, the majority of the ascent of Swyre Head is complete when the headland is reached.

On the grassy meadow at the top, some may wish to make use of the strategically placed stone bench by the path. Before turning to the left here across a stile, it is well worth continuing about a hundred yards to the other side of the headland to look down into the large cove of Chapman's Pool, which is a less dramatic version of Lulworth Cove. Then, crossing the stile by the bench, a path runs along by a wall through a high downland sheep pasture above Encombe down on the left. The lower house and farm is plainly in view and then, above the lake, the main house can be seen through the trees.

After a good mile from the cliff edge, the path bends to the right and then enters a wood. Here, it passes a couple of cottages on the right before crossing a crosstracks, marked on the left and right by private signs. The track then forks three ways: the right of way goes half right and out to the road near the village of Kingston at a small car park. Once on the road, turn to the left, away from the village, and follow it out of the wood and across a large arable field to a further small car park by the main entrance to the Encombe Estate on the left.

Once through the ornate gateway, the drive turns left and is marked with the characteristic Encombe Estate green private sign. The right of way, however, and route to the summit, goes straight ahead, through another gate and gently up across a field to the top of the scarp overlooking Encombe. Here, the track swings right and runs along the scarp top to reach the summit on the top of a large tumulus, although the trig point is away to the right at a slightly lower elevation. The coastal views are superb in both directions, with Purbeck's southern cliffs easily catching the eye. The Isle of Portland is also striking, appearing to rise from the sea as a lone monolith.

The descent path to Kimmeridge runs along the north-west ridge from the trig point, back further inland. It follows the edge of a first field before entering an enclosed track through what has been marked 'Heaven's Gate'. This track then traces the graceful curve of the top of the scarp around to Smedmore Hill, from where Smedmore House can be seen down on the left. Smedmore Hill is the final shoulder on the ridge before it drops down to the road above Kimmeridge. The track makes a steep descent and it is quickest to avoid other branching tracks on the left. When it does meet a small lane, a left turn leads out to the main road into Kimmeridge at the junction on the ridge crest, from where the quarry car park is just a few yards down on the left.

Hardown Hill

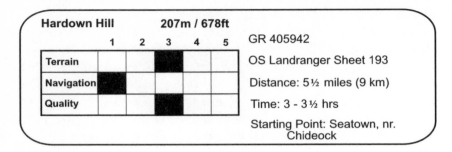

Hardown Hill	207m / 678ft				
	1	2	3	4	5
Terrain			■		
Navigation	■				
Quality			■		

GR 405942

OS Landranger Sheet 193

Distance: 5½ miles (9 km)

Time: 3 - 3½ hrs

Starting Point: Seatown, nr. Chideock

Hardown Hill is the most southerly of the hills within the main Wessex Downs ridge system. On its slopes, at mid height, it supports the village of Morecombelake, which is spread out along the popular A35 coast road between Lyme Regis and Bridport. The summit itself is a high heathland plateau, mainly covered with heather and gorse, but with a thick stand of bracken just below the summit level.

The best place to start a circular walk is the tiny village of Seatown, which can be reached down a narrow winding lane from Chideock on the A35. At Seatown, opposite the Anchor Inn, there is a large private car park, for which there is a daily charge; there are also toilets between the pub and beach. The route starts by following the lane back out of the village towards Chideock. Ignoring a first footpath on the left, a lane soon takes off to the left, signposted to Langdon Hill and to Seahill House. Beyond the house, which does bed and breakfast, it becomes a rough track and in due course joins with a track coming in at an acute angle from the right.

Beyond this, take the next track on the right, which contours around the slopes of Langdon Hill and reaches the entrance to another car park in the wood on the left. Continuing along its access road and then turning right at the end leads out onto the A35 at the top of Chideock Hill. Our route now leads to the left, although the A35 should soon be crossed where a grassy island in the middle makes it easier. After this, the village of Morecombelake is entered almost immediately and, just beyond the Esso garage on the left, a right turn should be made up a narrow lane, signposted to Ryall.

This lane continues through the upper part of the village, gradually climbing the slope, before meeting with another lane on the left; just beyond this, a tarmac driveway turns off to the left. Following this

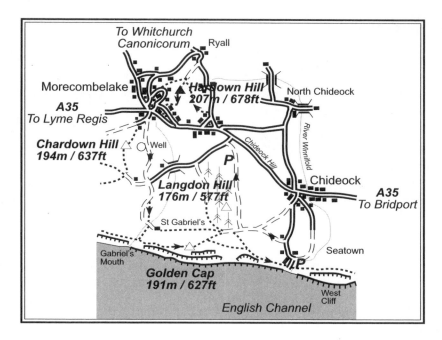

driveway initially and keeping straight on when the drive turns to the left, this path, overgrown with bracken and brambles in summer but still passable, leads up and past a water authority building before breaking out onto the open hill; it is here that the gorse starts. The thickets get denser as the path carries on, now traversing the upper eastern slopes but, ten thousand prickles later, the path emerges onto the heathery summit plateau.

The going now becomes noticeably easier as the path continues on to meet a wider, white-surfaced path that turns in from the left. Follow this to the left, up alongside an ancient earthwork until it reaches another junction marked by some dwarf gorse bushes. Ignoring a small path that crosses through the earthwork to the left, follow alongside the earthwork before turning left with it along another small path, not the track leading to the radio mast to the right. This path then leads up towards a stand of pine trees, which mark the highest point, although there is nothing on the ground to signify it.

The descent back into Morecombelake is significantly easier than the ascent. This path now leads on past the pine trees before swinging to the right and meeting the radio mast access track; this can then be followed to the left to reach another back lane in Morecombelake at a crossroads. Going straight on here, the lane leads down to the A35 again, a right turn on which then leads along to the Ship Inn. Opposite this, a small lane, named 'Ship Knap' then leads off, gently climbing the lower slopes of Chardown Hill.

In due course, a track slants off to the left, signposted to St Wite's Well and Golden Cap. St Wite's Well lies in the next field and is in a fenced enclosure, inside which grow a number of ornamental plants. The spring has been known since the 13th century and is believed to cure eye complaints. The byway then continues across the slopes of the hill before passing two houses and starting to descend to a crossroads at the end of a public road running across the valley on the left from the other end of Morecombelake.

Now aiming for Golden Cap, our route goes straight over and continues the descent down another rough road. Soon, a footpath takes off to the left through a gate and into a camping field, through which it follows the left-hand margin. It then crosses another field and then rejoins the track at the bottom of the small valley that runs out to the sea here. A left turn leads across the stream but a subsequent sharp right turn, on a path through the hedge, and then a further right turn, leads back across it. The track now underfoot then leads along parallel to the stream until it meets the South West Coast Path. Golden Cap is now towering up on the left and its ascent is next on the agenda. Turning towards it along the Coast Path, the path recrosses the stream and then leads along close to the top of the cliff.

A word of warning here: these cliffs are unstable and prone to landslides. In places, they are also undercut, so walking close to the edge on smaller paths, particularly on the top, is dangerous.

The route is now clear up the steepening hillside towards the summit, which is a ridge of a few hundred yards in length, marked with a trig point at the far end. The vast panorama from here is excellent. As well as the fine downland scenery inland, the coast can be seen in virtually an unbroken line from Portland to Seatown.

From the trig point, the descent to Seatown begins. The path runs down the upper slopes on the landward side of the ridge before entering the highest field through a gate. Here, the Coast Path turns to the right and then leads clearly back down the hill slope all the way to Seatown.

Nine Barrow Down

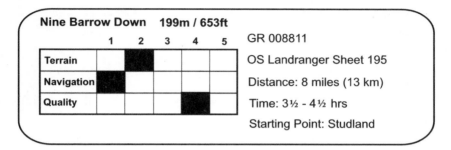

Nine Barrow Down	199m / 653ft					
	1	2	3	4	5	GR 008811
Terrain		■				OS Landranger Sheet 195
Navigation	■					Distance: 8 miles (13 km)
Quality				■		Time: 3½ - 4½ hrs
						Starting Point: Studland

Nine Barrow Down is the highest point on the most northerly of Purbeck's two ridges. Its status as a separate summit has been questioned, however, since the final few feet of the 492ft drop is provided by a cutting on the Swanage railway line. However, in view of the statements made in the introduction, it has been granted a worthy place in this book. Lying between Swanage and Studland, the hill can be climbed from either of these two places, although without doubt the best circuit can be made from Studland.

There are a number of appropriate parking areas in Studland, although the most convenient is close to the shore on the eastern side of the village. It can be reached down two lanes from the Shell Bay (Sandbanks Ferry) to Swanage road. If approaching from the ferry, take the first road on the left in the village, fork right and then turn right at a T-junction to reach the car park just before a pub. From Swanage or Corfe Castle, turn right at a crossroads just beyond the post office and, ignoring a turn on the left to the church, the car park is reached further down that road on the left just past the same pub mentioned above.

To begin, our route lies out along the clifftop of Handfast Point and Old Harry Rocks. Thus, walk down the road and past the pub to the toilet block on a right-hand bend. Once past the toilet block, turn to the left along a gently rising track that leads through the fields and out onto a clifftop meadow. The path runs through this, then through trees, to emerge once more on grassy turf close to Purbeck's easternmost point. Old Harry is in fact a large detached sea stack at the point, containing a natural arch. The next headland around the corner is also cut by an archway, which is best viewed from the promontory beyond that. More promontories follow, two of which have detached stacks, and all are worth

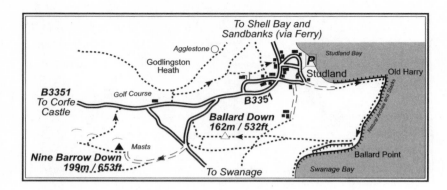

a look. To get the best view of them, it is necessary to follow the cliff edge path rather than the other broader one a little further inland, from where the best of the coastal scenery is hidden.

Ahead, the tracks rise gently up towards Ballard Point. Here, at a large cliff, the main chalk ridge gives way to the waves until it appears again at the Needles on the Isle of Wight, which can be seen across the water to the east. At Ballard Point, the coast turns slightly to the right and shortly beyond this the path forks. The right-hand fork leads past the trig point, which is not the summit of the down, and on along the high chalk ridge. Swanage is prominent in the view to the left, whilst Poole Harbour, Brownsea Island and Studland Heath all catch the eye in the northwards direction. In due course, the highest point of the gently rising ridge of Ballard Down is reached, although it is unadorned by any landmark other than a lump of old concrete, which serves only as a rather uncomfortable seat.

The ridge, however, continues and begins its descent to the obelisk further down the ridge through a gate. At the obelisk, which, as a significant landmark, was demolished during the war and then rebuilt in peacetime, turn to the left down a steep path that drops down interminable steps to the foot of the steep hillside. Here, it meets another path, the Purbeck Way, which began at Ballard Point and has taken a different route across the hillside to this point. A right turn on this path leads along the verdant lower slopes to a stile out onto the Studland to Swanage road.

On the other side, however, the ground rises steeply once again, this time to Nine Barrow Down. Slightly to the left, the Purbeck Way continues across the road and into a field. Here, it curves to the left to pick up a broader track that is followed onwards and upwards. To begin with, it climbs out of the combe in which it starts before climbing along the Swanage slopes of the Down to reach the ridge beyond the masts in a large upland pasture. Here, the path turns sharply to the left but the trig point can be reached on the far side of the field by aiming half left.

The route back to Studland begins by rejoining the path on the other side of the field and following that westwards away from Ballard Down. It leads into a further field, where it starts to descend slightly with the ridge but, at the lowest point, a gate on the right marks the beginning of another path. This turns half right through the gate and drops down to the top of the wood at the bottom of this next field. The path then follows along the outer edge of this wood before entering it through a gate and dropping down the hillside within it.

By the time the bottom of the wood is reached, the descent is almost complete and a path then leads out along the edge of a couple of fields to the Corfe Castle to Studland road. A short stretch of roadwalking then follows along that to the right before access can be gained to Studland Heath. First, there is the Swanage road on the right and then the golf course's clubhouse and car park on the left. After that, there is a tricky section of narrow and slightly sunken road before a small lay-by and bridleway are reached on the left.

This bridleway cuts through some scrub to reach a junction of paths on the edge of the heath and golf course. A right turn here, signposted to Studland Village, leads along another bridleway that cuts down the edge of the golf course and then through the heath proper, affording good views of the large detached rock known as the Agglestone over to the left. However, when the bridleway turns sharply to the left, keep ahead on a path over a stile that continues to some houses at the back of Studland that adjoin the heath. A rough road runs along the front of this row of houses before turning sharply to the right at the far end. Here again, keep straight on along the path, ignoring a bridleway on the left and then going left at a fork to reach a further junction of paths.

We are now not too far distant from Studland village itself and it is most conveniently reached by turning to the left down a large bridlepath and, ignoring parallel paths on the left, turning sharply back right over a stile in the hedge into a horse paddock. The path crosses over this to the far corner, where it joins the head of a rough track that runs out to the main road in the village. Here, turn right and then left down a small lane just beyond the bus stop. Soon, take the right fork by a deep pond and then follow this down to a T-junction. A right turn there leads back to the car park and pub.

Section 4 – South-east England

The Solent from Portsmouth and Southampton Water to the Itchen. That river to its source at Preston Candover. The B3046 from there to Basingstoke and the River Lodden from there to the Thames at Shiplake. The River Thames to Wallingford and the chalk escarpment to Luton. The River Lea from there to Hackney and the Thames from there to the sea. The coastline of Kent, East and West Sussex and Hampshire to Portsmouth.

NAME	HEIGHT	IN SECTION	IN ENGLAND	IN BRITAIN
Leith Hill	295m / 968ft	01 of 13	141 of 184	1382J of 1552
Black Down	280m / 919ft	02 of 13	145 of 184	1412 of 1552
Butser Hill	270m / 887ft	03 of 13	151 of 184	1427 of 1552
Wendover Woods	267m / 876ft	04 of 13	155 of 184	1433 of 1552
Botley Hill	267m / 875ft	05 of 13	156 of 184	1434 of 1552
Ditchling Beacon	248m / 813ft	06 of 13	162 of 184	1467J of 1552
Crowborough	242m / 794ft	07 of 13	165 of 184	1473 of 1552
Chanctonbury Hill	238m / 782ft	08 of 13	167 of 184	1477 of 1552
Firle Beacon	217m / 713ft	09 of 13	172 of 184	1496J of 1552
Wilmington Hill	214m / 702ft	10 of 13	174 of 184	1502 of 1552
Castle Hill	200m / 656ft	11 of 13	178 of 184	1517 of 1552
Cheriton Hill	188m / 617ft	12 of 13	180 of 184	1528 of 1552
Cliffe Hill	164m / 538ft	13 of 13	184 of 184	1547 of 1552

There are few places in the world with as great a diversity of landscapes as the Weald of south-east England. Within this small corner of the country, the scenery varies in as little as a few miles from thick pinewoods and sandy heaths to wet clay vales and curving chalk crests. Although a densely populated area of the country, much of the Weald remains relatively unspoilt with some areas being very quiet, rural and, in some cases, wild and rough.

The Weald is constructed from the Cretaceous series of rocks, deposited

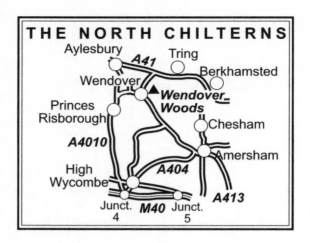

THE NORTH CHILTERNS

Aylesbury · A41 · Tring · Berkhamsted · Wendover · Wendover Woods · Princes Risborough · A4010 · Chesham · High Wycombe · A404 · Amersham · A413 · Junct. 4 · M40 · Junct. 5

between 65 and 146 million years ago when dinosaurs roamed the earth. At the beginning of this time, a vast floodplain existed across south-east England – the Wessex Basin – and over north-eastern France – the Paris Basin. Rivers meandered across the plain from the uplands to the north – the London Platform – and the Amorican Massif to the south over the central part of northern France.

These rivers deposited sandy, deltaic beds whilst the currents flowed fast as the land was uplifted. When this ceased, the currents slowed and vast mudbanks formed over the delta. This gave rise to a cyclical sequence of clays and sandstones, with the sandstones becoming increasingly bedded and tough as time proceeded. The first cycle consists of the Fairlight Clay and Ashdown Beds, which together form the Hastings Beds. The sands of the latter form the central portion of the High Weald and the Fairlight Clay causes the slumps in the cliffs at Hastings as water enters the clay layers and allows them to slide relative to each other, carrying seawards whatever lies above them.

Next came the Wadhurst Clay, a calcareous mixture of shales, sandstones and limestones, rather than a true, weakly compacted mudstone. This layer is rich in ironstones, whose ores gave rise to the prosperous iron industry of the Weald (see below). Above that, the first tough sandstones appear – the Lower and Upper Tunbridge Wells Sands, separated by the Grinstead Clay. The toughest of the Tunbridge Wells Sands, the Ardingly Sandstone is so resistant that it is able to form large cliffs along valley sides, thus producing the only large exposures of really

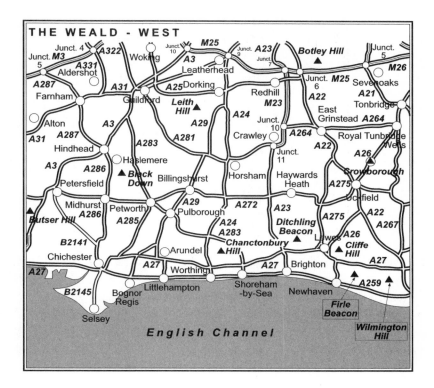

THE WEALD - WEST

solid rock in much of south-eastern England and the Midlands. Most people know little of these cliffs, some of which support caves, spires and chimneys, although those around Tunbridge Wells are more famous.

The final cyclothem is dominated by clays – the thick Lower and Upper Weald Clays, although they too are separated by a thin sandstone – the Horsham Stone, which is much prized for its strong but heavy roofing flags. Following this large thick layer of clay is another sandstone, which was deposited in marine conditions as the sea once more covered much of Britain. This sandstone is known as the Lower Greensand and after an initial thin layer – the Atherfield Clay – the Hythe Beds were deposited. These vary in their composition across the Weald and the soft sands that exist in Kent are much favoured by fruit growers whilst further west the Hythe Beds contain much stronger rocks that help form the steep escarpment of the Greensand Ridge (see below). The toughness results from layers of a type of quartz, known as chert, and it is these layers that give rise to some of the highest ground in the Weald.

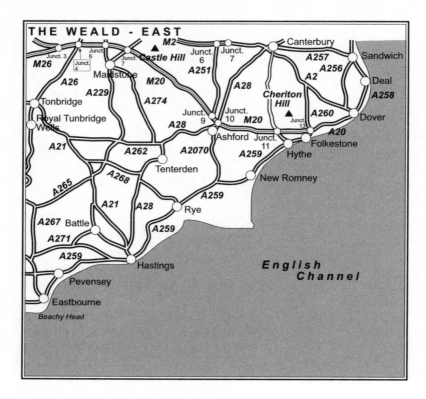

THE WEALD - EAST

Volcanic activity further to the west, associated with the opening of the Atlantic Ocean, threw out ash into the air and this appears in the Lower Greensand strata as thin beds of clay. In the past, this was used, due to its absorbent properties, to remove grease from sheeps' wool. This process is known as fulling and hence the sticky clay has become known as Fuller's earth. Reigate was a major centre for its extraction.

The middle beds of the Lower Greensand are known as the Sandgate Beds and, together with the Folkestone Beds above them, they are named, like the Hythe Beds, after the Kent coastal towns where they are exposed in the sea cliffs. The Folkestone Beds are, like the Wadhurst Clay, rich in iron, although they are not as tough as the Hythe Beds. However, a thin band of very resistant carstone forms the topmost layer of the Folkestone Beds and that does remain in places as a capping.

As the sea deepened and joined with the Yorkshire Basin through a channel known as the Bedfordshire Straits, the deposition shifted back towards clay. The result was a thin layer of dark Gault Clay before sandstones were once more deposited as a much less tough material, the Upper Greensand. The name greensand is derived from the green colour of hydrated potassium iron silicate, or glauconite, which is more prominent in the Upper Greensand rather than in the Lower Greensand where it tends to have been oxidised to a greater extent leading to a more yellow colour.

Further subsidence of the land surface allowed this sea to deepen and spread over the whole of Britain. This shallow clear sea was home to a large population of small scaly creatures called coccolithophores – a tiny plankton. Their corpses collected on the sea floor and their scales, coccoliths, compacted to form a very pure limestone sequence; this is the chalk itself. The chalk is discussed in more detail in Section 3 where it is most prominent in the landscape.

The Cretaceous period came to an end with the massive extinction that wiped out the dinosaurs, which is believed to be due, at least in part, to the collision of a comet with the earth in southern Mexico. This heralded the beginning of the Tertiary period when the opening of the Atlantic Ocean led to a doming of western Britain, causing a north-west to south-east dip and forcing the retreat of the shallow chalk-depositing sea that was covering Britain. The chalk and greensands were then eroded from much of the resulting highlands of western and northern Britain, being confined only to the southern and eastern fringes of England.

The same period also saw Africa collide into southern Europe, crumpling the crust and building the massive mountains of the Alps. This orogeny, or mountain building episode, was not, however, confined to the Alps. The crust of southern England was also crumpled and this affected the Wealden beds and subsequent strata. This lateral pressure formed a huge mountain with its summit somewhere over the top of Crowborough. Neighbouring synclines also formed in Hampshire (see Section 3) and at London and in these basins Tertiary deposits formed.

A radial drainage system came into being on the chalk slopes of the Wealden dome and subsequent erosion had the effect of effectively slicing off the top so that all the geological formations are exposed on the surface. Differing rates of erosion have given rise to concentric circular ridges and vales. Outermost is the chalk, which forms the North and South Downs, and this is separated from the Greensand Ridge by a vale formed from the less resistant Upper Greensand and Gault Clay. Inside the Lower

Greensand, the thick clay bed of the Lower and Upper Wealden Clays has given rise to a wide trough, known as the Low Weald. Finally, the land rises through a complex terrain due to the clays and sandstones of the Hastings Beds to the highest point of the High Weald at Crowborough.

However, rather than following these natural valleys, the swift radially flowing rivers superimposed themselves on the lower strata as they cut down through the chalk to form breaches in the greensand and chalk downland. Take the Medway, for example. It rises close to East Grinstead on the High Weald and flows down onto the Low Weald at Tonbridge. From here, it cuts through the Greensand Ridge at the small village of Yalding to reach the town of Maidstone at the foot of the chalk escarpment. At Maidstone, the river becomes tidal as it slices a deep gash in the North Downs to reach the sea at Rochester.

It is the rapidly changing succession of sands and clays across the Weald inside the chalk that gives rise to the large scenic changes across the region. Moving southwards from the North Downs, the fertile but dry chalk downland falls in a steep escarpment to the Vale of Holmwood. Here, the A25 makes its way along the Gault Clay vale avoiding the high ground to the north and south. Very quickly and normally within a couple of miles of the foot of the chalk scarp, sometimes as little as a few hundred yards, the ground starts to rise gently up the Lower Greensand dipslope.

The traveller is now presented with a completely different scene. Thick pine woods, such as the Hurtwood at Holmbury St Mary, stand alongside heaths of heather and sand, such as Frensham and Thursley Commons, giving a Scottish feel to this small corner of England. The tough chert beds give Leith Hill its prominence as the highest hill in south-eastern England, presiding over some of the poorest soils in England.

A further steep escarpment then falls to the Low Weald. Here, thick clay soils that are difficult to plough are given over to permanent grassland and oak woodland. Traditionally, roads skirt the Low Weald where possible and cross it quickly and directly where necessary, as, before surfaced roads became the norm, tracks soon become impassable to most traffic. Narrow twisting valleys in the clay beds and sandstone ridges dominate the rise onto the High Weald. The scenery on the sandstone is similar to that of the greensand and, at Ashdown Forest, heathlands once more prevail.

Southwards, the journey continues in reverse as the descent off the

High Weald leads onto the wet clay of the Low Weald. Here, however, the Lower Greensand is much thinner and forms a lower and much less prominent ridge that is completely overshadowed by the imposing scarp slope of the South Downs. Most travellers across the region, however, notice little of the best effects of the changing scene as the major roads prefer the radial river valleys to other switchback routes over the hills.

By the time the Weald was formed, however, England was still joined to France at Dover, as a large inlet that would become the English Channel was separated from the North Sea by the chalk and Wealden Beds. At the end of the Ice Age, meltwaters from Scandinavia, eastern Scotland, northern England and the Baltic flowed into the large basin of the North Sea. The ice sheet blocked off the northern exit and the water level rose until it breached the chalk at Dover and carved a deep channel to form the British Isles.

The water also sliced off part of the Wealden structure between Hythe and Eastbourne so that west of Dover's famous white cliffs are the smaller greensand cliffs at Hythe and Folkestone. These are followed by the low bank of the Low Weald at places such as Hamstreet before the High Weald forms the shore at Rye and Hastings. West of Hastings, the Pevensey Levels have formed on the Low Weald before the South Downs terminate high above the sea in the massive chalk cliffs of Beachy Head. The lack of mention of the greensand between the Low Weald and the South Downs is not an omission as its beds are so thin hereabouts that they cease to exist at Polegate where the Low Weald meets the Gault. A subsequent fall in sea level, coupled with deposition behind the shingle spit at Dungeness, formed Romney Marsh and left the old shoreline cliffs – the Saxon Shore – far inland with old ports like Rye and Appledore dry.

Northwards from the summit of the North Downs the dipslope falls away down to the London Basin and only reappears out of the Basin's Tertiary deposits at the foot of the Chiltern dipslope, which faces the dipslope of the North Downs on the other side of the London Basin. The Basin continues as far west as Reading and Newbury before the Chilterns and their continuation – the North Wessex Downs – are united with the Wessex Downs (Section 3), which the North Downs joined at the western end of the Weald at Alton.

The Chilterns, however, are not simply an extension of the Wessex Downs. In fact, the deep valley of the Thames at Goring Gap separates the two. The Gap is thought to have been formed by meltwaters from an early ice age in a similar way to the Channel at Dover, although on a smaller scale. The Chilterns are famous for their beechwoods, which are in complete contrast to the traditional open pastures of the other downland. The difference is, however, due to a thick capping of Tertiary clay, which is discussed in Section 3.

As mentioned earlier, the Wealden beds contain deposits of iron, notably in the Wadhurst Clay and the lower greensand. The earliest reference to iron extraction is during the Roman period when the Weald was an important mining area. In 1496, England's first blast furnace was constructed in Ashdown Forest and, due to the plentiful supply of smelting materials, the industry blossomed to reach its peak in the late part of the 16th century when well over a hundred blast furnaces were in operation. Demand was fuelled by the need to produce iron guns and cannon for an increasing number of naval conflicts. Various methods, from mines to small open-cast operations, were used to extract the ore.

Blast furnaces are constructed from special heat-resistant bricks and in it the iron ore, usually in the form of haematite (iron oxide), is reduced (de-oxidised) to iron. The reaction starts by igniting a source of carbon, which, in the Weald, was normally charcoal (obtained from the local forests), with a blast of hot air to oxidise it to the toxic gas carbon monoxide (CO):

$$\text{carbon} + \text{oxygen} \rightarrow \text{carbon monoxide}$$

A lack in the quantity of air supplied prevents the full oxidation to the common and harmless gas carbon dioxide (CO_2). However, carbon monoxide is what is known as a reducing agent and it thus proceeds to reduce ('de-oxidise') the iron ore to iron:

$$\textbf{iron ore} \text{ (haematite)} + \text{carbon monoxide} \rightarrow \text{iron} + \text{carbon dioxide}$$

Meanwhile, other molten impurities collect at the bottom of the furnace and these are made into a slag by reacting them with quicklime, CaO. This is easily produced by adding limestone or local chalk to the furnace at the start of the process; heat decomposes limestone to quicklime:

$$\text{limestone} + \text{heat} \rightarrow \text{quicklime} + \text{carbon dioxide}$$

In total, it could be expected that seven tonnes of iron could be obtained from each ten tonnes of haematite, although as the ore was only around 5 to 10 per cent, it was necessary to mine about 20 tonnes of ore to get just a tonne of iron.

The thick wet clay soils of the Weald have traditionally been given over to permanent oak woodland and thus there was a plentiful supply of wood from which to make charcoal. Limestone can be found in the Wealden Beds and, at the centre of the Wealden anticline, there is a small exposure of the Jurassic Purbeck limestone (see Sections 3 and 5). However, the chalk that bounds the Weald is the most plentiful source of calcium carbonate, whilst the narrow Wealden valleys were dammed to form hammer ponds providing water to drive the forge hammers and water-wheels that were used in the crushing and separation of the ore from the waste rock and clay. The separation process culminated in allowing the ore to settle out in water, where, being heavier, it sank first before the other lighter waste material.

The demise of the Wealden industry was due in part to cheaper Swedish imports, although the adoption of iron weaponry by the navy, as mentioned above, saved the industry at least for some time. However, it was cheaper to use coke to smelt the iron instead of charcoal and thus, finally, the industry collapsed in favour of the lower grade iron ore found around the English coalfields; the last furnace at Ashburnham closed in 1830.

Today, with the iron pits filled in or flooded and much of the oak woodland that supported them felled to provide farmland that could be drained to give some productive output, the Weald was left as it is now. The high crest of chalk surrounds the Weald and forms the summits of Butser Hill, Ditchling Beacon, Chanctonbury Hill, Firle Beacon, Wilmington Hill and Cliffe Hill on the South Downs, from whose summits their sister summits on the North Downs – Botley Hill, Castle Hill and Cheriton Hill – can be seen on a clear day. Across the Gault Clay vale, the tough sandstones form the highest summit of all, Leith Hill, closely followed by the second, Black Down, at Haslemere. In the centre of the anticline, the summit of the High Weald lies amongst the suburban streets of Crowborough, alongside the heathland of Ashdown Forest. Finally, northwards from the North Downs and across the prosperous valley of the Thames, the beech-clad Chilterns attain their highest point in Wendover Woods.

Accommodation

South-east England is, despite the large commuter conurbations, a reasonably popular tourist destination, with many parts of the Weald being regarded as prominent beauty spots and honey pots, although, with such a large local population, many of the visitors are day trippers from London and other nearby towns. However, there is a variety of accommodation from large hotels in the seaside resorts, such as Brighton, Hove and Hastings to bed and breakfast in cottages and farms located in tranquil downland villages. Further inland, picturesque towns like Rye, Tenterden and Tunbridge Wells provide plentiful accommodation both in the towns and the surrounding villages. There are youth hostels at Bradenham (between Princes Risborough and High Wycombe), Jordans (near Chalfont St Giles), Windsor, Tanners Hatch (near Dorking), Holmbury St Mary, Hindhead, Kemsing, Medway (near Chatham), Canterbury, Margate, Broadstairs, Dover, Hastings, Eastbourne, Alfriston, Telscombe, Brighton, Truleigh Hill (near Shoreham-on-Sea), Portsmouth and Blackboys (near Buxted).

Leith Hill

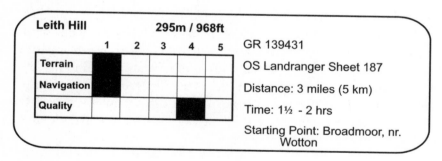

Leith Hill	1	2	3	4	5	295m / 968ft
Terrain	■					GR 139431
Navigation	■					OS Landranger Sheet 187
Quality				■		Distance: 3 miles (5 km)
						Time: 1½ - 2 hrs
						Starting Point: Broadmoor, nr. Wotton

Leith Hill is the highest point on the Greensand Ridge and lies geographically between Dorking and Horsham. It is normally approached from a car park to the west, a short distance below the summit, although an approach from the north is much more interesting and more pleasing.

The ascent begins from the small and little-known hamlet of

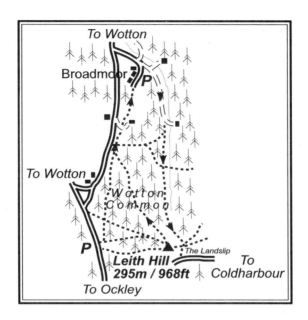

To Wotton

Broadmoor P

To Wotton

Wotton Common

P

The Landslip

Leith Hill 295m / 968ft

To Coldharbour

To Ockley

Broadmoor. This is approached from the A25 at Wotton down a small lane, named Sheephouse Lane but otherwise unsignposted, next to the Wotton Hatch Inn, which is open for food during the day. After about two miles, take a dead-end lane on the left, signposted to Broadmoor, which, after descending a steep hill, enters the hamlet and runs up to a telephone kiosk and post box.

There is parking on either side of the telephone box for about six or seven cars and it is from here that the walk begins. Start by walking back down the road for a few hundred yards until it bends around to the left. Here, turn right on a rough lane, which is the access road to a number of cottages and houses that lie in the wood. After a short distance, fork right again and continue straight ahead up the lane, ignoring footpaths leading up the hill on the right and tracks leading to houses on the left.

In a while, the main lane bends around to the left and here walk straight ahead up a smaller path. Again ignoring any paths leading off on either side, continue up the small valley, through an area of acid scrubland and Scots pine trees, all the way to the ridge, where a much larger path is met.

A right turn on this leads straight up the hill to the trig point and tower on the summit. It is possible to gain the best view by climbing the tower, hence getting above the trees. This is possible between April and October and Sundays in winter; this is free to National Trust members but there is a small charge for other members of the public. There is also a small snack bar.

On a warm day, the summit is a popular picnic site and the hill itself is very busy. However, by again descending onto the northern slopes, most of the crowds are left behind. Continue on past the tower and then immediately fork right. Now, ignoring a path on the left, this track leads on through the woodland on Wotton Common, which is interspersed with rhododendron thickets. Soon a much larger track is joined, which should be followed to the right and over two crosstracks. After the second, a gravelled lane is followed downhill, although this should soon be left on the left (signposted) when it starts to climb uphill. The path now leads onwards down a small valley before reaching the end of the public road at Broadmoor; the lay-by is now only a short distance further on.

Black Down

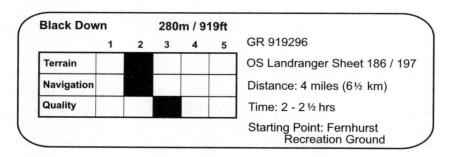

Black Down	1	2	3	4	5	280m / 919ft
Terrain		■				GR 919296
Navigation		■				OS Landranger Sheet 186 / 197
Quality			■			Distance: 4 miles (6½ km)

GR 919296

OS Landranger Sheet 186 / 197

Distance: 4 miles (6½ km)

Time: 2 - 2 ½ hrs

Starting Point: Fernhurst Recreation Ground

Black Down stands on the greensand of Haslemere and has very different vegetation from other parts of the south. This interesting walk climbs through the small eroded valleys into a pinewood on the top of the hill which seems very high above its surrounding landscape. The lower ground can be particularly muddy and difficult in the winter.

Begin at the recreation ground car park in Fernhurst, by the village green next to the Red Lion, which is open for lunchtime and evening meals every day. Leave the car park by walking past the sports changing-rooms (where the toilets may be open) and, once behind them, turn left

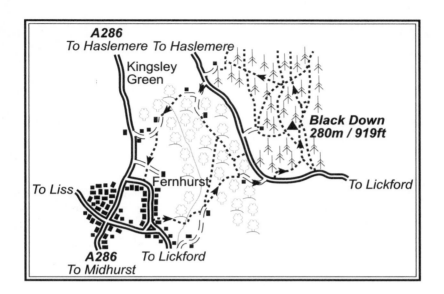

and follow the fence to the path running along the northern edge of the pitch. Turn right on this path, pass through a gate and follow it uphill until it comes to a track by some buildings. Turn left on this track, keeping straight on where the main track goes left after about a hundred yards. This path leads up through the woods to a driveway, which should be followed to reach the public road running around the hill. Turn right and almost immediately turn half left up a track soon turning left on a steeply rising sunken bridleway. When this reaches a seat near the top of the hill, turn back half left and walk up a wide track, which soon comes to a T-junction. Here, turn right and follow the path around to the left. A path soon joins from the right (running obliquely back); keep straight on for exactly one hundred yards where a left turn up the bank (no path) should be made. A little exploration will reveal the trig point amongst the pine trees and small depressions.

Return to the track and turn left for a short distance. After passing another track coming in on the right, and some steps leading downhill on the right, turn left on a bridleway and then keep straight on over a crosstracks. Shortly, the track bears right but, instead of following it, follow a slightly sunken track keeping straight on which leads on to reach another track (the Sussex Border Path). Turn left, shortly bearing half right at a large junction (signposted Sussex Border Path). Keep straight on over two crosstracks then shortly after the second, bear left at a fork onto a bridleway running downhill. Soon, turn sharp back left, downhill, on another sunken bridleway, which leads down to Valewood House.

Turn left on its drive but, instead of following the drive to the right, follow the bridleway ahead which leads to the road. Turn left on the road, and shortly turn right on a tarmacked drive. Follow this uphill and then quite steeply downhill before turning right on a track. Follow this across a small valley, ignoring two paths on the right, past a very nice house on the right before reaching another driveway. Follow this tarmacked road past a large house on the right before turning left through a gate as the road bends slightly to the right. Follow this path downhill, crossing a farm road, into the back of the village. When the road is met in Fernhurst, turn left and follow it back down past the Red Lion to the recreation ground.

Butser Hill

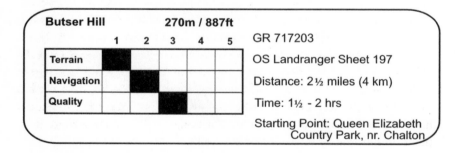

Butser Hill			270m / 887ft			
	1	2	3	4	5	
Terrain	■					
Navigation		■				
Quality			■			

GR 717203

OS Landranger Sheet 197

Distance: 2½ miles (4 km)

Time: 1½ - 2 hrs

Starting Point: Queen Elizabeth Country Park, nr. Chalton

Butser Hill is the most westerly separate summit of the South Downs and holds a commanding position, rising steeply from the A3 London to Portsmouth dual carriageway. The radio mast on its summit apart, it is a fine hill with its traditional downland scenery and flora little changed by modern agriculture, although no doubt this is partly due to the fact that a large part of it lies within the boundaries of the Queen Elizabeth Country Park.

In fact, it is from the park's visitor centre, with all facilities, that the ascent is best commenced. A truly circular route is difficult and impractical but a token circuit can be made around the head of a small combe on the hill's south-eastern slopes.

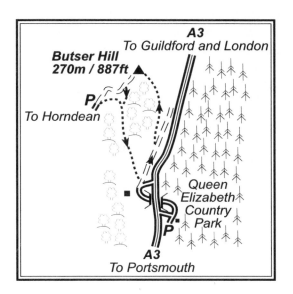

The Queen Elizabeth Country Park is signposted off the A3 between Horndean and Petersfield and there are sliproads on both carriageways.

The car park itself is pay-and-display, which incidently is more expensive on a Sunday than on a Saturday. On a fine day, however, the car park is not quite large enough and space becomes very limited with the park's other car parks being distant, spread out along the forest trail on the opposite slopes of the valley from Butser Hill. Those approaching the hill from the south should ignore earlier signs to Butser Hill as these direct the motorist to the summit car park and, although much easier, a route from there cannot exactly be described as a walk.

From the Country Park car park, walk back out onto the access road and turn to the right. The South Downs Way is now joined and it leads through a tunnel before crossing the road on the far side and crossing some rough ground; at this stage the route is well waymarked by blue-topped stakes, intended for horse riders. After dropping down from the dual carriageway, the track enters valley pasture in Hillhampton Bottom before beginning to ascend the hill's slopes.

At this point, leave the path and continue along the edge of the field, below the dual carriageway, until a track is found entering the field on the right; now follow this along and through a gate into the next field. A grassy path can now be seen clearly ascending the hill's slopes just to the right of the combe, with its traditional vegetation of yew trees. When almost at the top of the slope, there is a gate, beyond which the route becomes indistinct. However, do not aim for the top of the unsightly mast but instead aim between the two copses of trees whose tops can be seen. When between them, the beacon will be seen ahead; the trig point is a short distance to its right. On a clear day, the view is spectacular, the South Downs being seen almost in their entirety.

The descent begins by walking towards the radio mast and passing through the gate on its left-hand side. Ahead lies the mast's access road (which leads to the summit car park) but our route takes us half left along a small grassy path, leading around the head of the combe and down to a gate at the top of the next ridge. Beyond, a wide grassy track, similar to the one used on the ascent, drops steeply back down to Hillhampton Bottom where the outwards route is rejoined close to the car park.

Wendover Woods

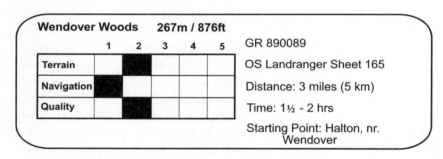

Wendover Woods	267m / 876ft				
	1	2	3	4	5
Terrain		■			
Navigation	■				
Quality		■			

GR 890089

OS Landranger Sheet 165

Distance: 3 miles (5 km)

Time: 1½ - 2 hrs

Starting Point: Halton, nr. Wendover

Within Wendover Woods lies the highest point in the Chiltern Hills, which are renowned for their beechwoods. These woods are, however, a forestry plantation, consisting of beech and conifer trees, which cover all of this part of the escarpment. The woodlands are accessible by car and in the middle of them, close to the top, there is a large pay-and-display car park with double charges at weekends. This walk should be done in winter when there are no leaves on the trees and the views can be seen through the branches.

Begin the walk from near the Halton RAF Camp. From Wendover, leave the town by the main road to Tring. Keep on the main road through the

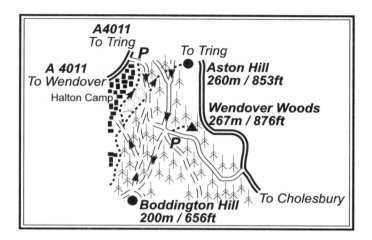

outskirts of Halton village and pass the derestriction sign. At a crossroad sign, turn right through a narrow gate with a 20 mph sign and park on the left rather than entering the Mansion Hill estate. This is a small parking area with no facilities but also with no charge. From Tring, before arriving at Wendover, the road to Aston Hill and Buckland Common is passed on the left as is the Chiltern Forestry Office, before turning left.

Leave by the track running roughly east up into the plantation. This soon turns right and becomes a sunken trackway. About one-third of the way up the hill, turn sharply back left on a path going up some steps with a flint retaining wall on the uphill side. Follow this up and cross straight over the tarmacked road leading to the car park. Beyond here, go ahead on the level at the first fork and then right and uphill at the second to reach another track which again should be crossed straight over into a field via a stile. The trig point is in the middle of this field. Although this is not actually the highest point, it does give the best views, being out of the wood. Return to the stile and turn left on the track. This soon reaches the tarmacked road – keep straight on – and the car park is soon reached. In the car park, turn left (signposted 'Chiltern Highest Point'). Soon, take a left fork, which leads to a stone on the edge of the trees; this marks the summit.

Return to the car park and turn left and then right (signposted 'Fitness Trail' and later to 'Boddington Hill Walk'). Follow this down to the edge of the ancient hill fort at Boddington, which can be explored if desired. Turn sharp right back down a broad grassy track and descend increasingly steeply, keeping left, down to a gate to the RAF Camp. Turn right before the gate, following a bridleway that runs at a more or less even gradient across the hill. Ignore a path running steeply up the hill to the right and continue on to reach another sunken lane. Turn left and follow the lane again to the edge of the camp. Keep along the bottom of the wood and continue straight on forking left off the bridleway onto a footpath and then joining it again to reach the track used on the ascent, only a short distance from where the car was left.

Botley Hill

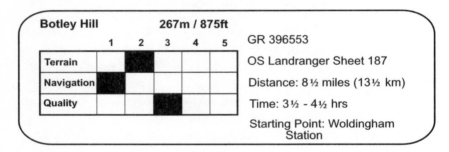

Botley Hill		267m / 875ft			
	1	2	3	4	5
Terrain		■			
Navigation	■				
Quality			■		

GR 396553

OS Landranger Sheet 187

Distance: 8½ miles (13½ km)

Time: 3½ - 4½ hrs

Starting Point: Woldingham Station

Botley Hill is the highest point of the North Downs and lies on the edge of London's suburbia, between the towns of Caterham and Oxted. This route is probably one of the more strenuous described in the book as the North Downs ridge is crossed over twice, with a descent nearly to valley level on the far side. That said, the route makes an excellent and varied, albeit long, walk, best enjoyed on a warm and fine day.

The start of the route is at the station car park in the commuter village of Woldingham, with its large houses spread out over a large area of green and leafy side roads. It is free to park in the station car park at weekends and bank holidays but, during the week, it is quite possible to park on the side road leading to Church Road Farm next to the station. Of course, it is also possible to arrive by train and there is a regular daily service through the station between Victoria and East Grinstead. There is a branch line between Oxted, Crowborough and Uckfield.

Leave the station by walking up the side road mentioned above until there is a bridge over the railway line on the right. Cross this and then walk

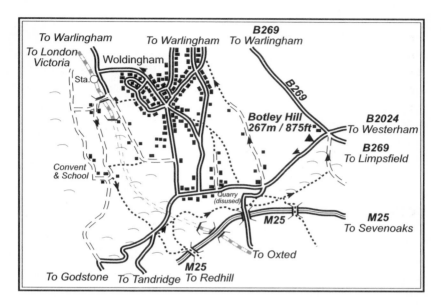

up the metalled road beyond to, and then through, the farm at Marden Park. Keeping straight on, the lane, which is a bridleway, becomes increasingly muddy as the clay has been churned up by the many horses that clearly pass this way. After a gentle uphill walk, the lane reaches the complex of buildings at the convent school run by the Sacred Heart Foundation.

Here, keep straight on past the small cemetery on the left to reach a stile. Cross over this and follow a path that starts to climb more steeply uphill and stays on the left-hand side of the field beyond. Towards the top of the field, woodland appears on the left and, in the top left-hand corner, the path crosses a stile and enters the woodland. Although there are numerous paths leading off to the left and right, keep straight ahead at all junctions, following the small waymarkers for the Woldingham Countryside Walk. The track eventually reaches a road junction on the crest of the ridge just after passing a noticeboard provided by the Woodland Trust who own the woodland hereabouts at Marden Park.

A left turn on the road leads through the junction and the North Downs Way is then joined. The next section of the route follows the North Downs Way as we descend the southern escarpment of the ridge. There are few navigational problems on this section, as the Countryside Commission's acorn fingerposts mark every junction, but a description is given nonetheless.

Following the road east, the route soon takes off down a track on the right that runs roughly parallel to and slightly below the road for the time being. Soon, it drops down further to the right before turning back to run along the hillside then reaching the top of a long flight of steps on the right. Go down the steps and once the trees are left behind, a viewing platform constructed in 1999 is on the left. It can now be seen that our route is descending directly above the railway tunnel, which runs under the downs between Woldingham and Oxted.

The descent continues down a few more steps before the path bends sharply to the left and narrows as it runs along the hillside through small thickets and open grass downland. In due course, though, it comes up against the western boundary of a large quarry hereabouts and the path is forced downhill almost as far as the M25. Finally, the path runs along the bottom of the quarry-owned land and passes a house before emerging onto the Oxted and Woldingham road. A short distance down this road to the right, the North Downs Way takes off on the left and climbs uphill and over a stile. Just after this there is a fork and, although the North Downs Way keeps straight ahead, a quick shortcut can be made by going right and rejoining the 'official' route in about a hundred yards.

The path now runs along the bottom of the slope of downland grassland before meeting the Vanguard Way at a stile at the far side. Over this and then soon over another, the end of the last of the five North Downs Way–Greensand Way links is found, but our route continues straight on along the bottom of a wood to reach a sunken chalk lane at the far end. Here, the route goes left, up the lane, and through the woodland, here owned by the Titsey Foundation; the main Warlingham to Westerham road is met on the ridge at the top.

Start by going left and then left again down a side road named 'The Ridge'. We are now very close to the summit of the hill and soon the trig point is to be found just into the field on the right. The descent back to Woldingham begins by following the road straight ahead for about a mile until a road to Oxted is found descending the escarpment on the left. At this point, which is actually a sort of crossroads, turn right up a small private lane that passes by a number of houses. Soon, the tarmac swings around to the right but follow the bridleway, which keeps straight on along a gravelled track. This stretches for quite a way through woodland but, when the track swings left to a gate, go straight on down a smaller path through the woodland to emerge onto the open hill above Woldingham. A descent down the hill now leads to one of the village's many roads.

Although now back in Woldingham, the village is very spread out and the station is still quite a distance away. A left turn on the road soon leads uphill and over a crossroads. At the top of the hill, just before the 30 mph speed restriction sign, turn sharp back right down a road that passes a number of fine houses to arrive at the Edwardian frontage of Woldingham House. In front of it, turn left down Croft Road, which leads all the way to the main road in the village next to the church. A right turn now leads down the long hill to the station at the very bottom.

Ditchling Beacon

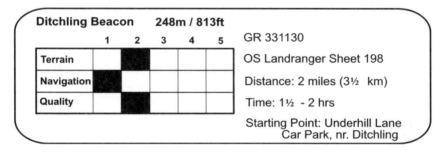

Ditchling Beacon	248m / 813ft				
	1	2	3	4	5
Terrain		■			
Navigation	■				
Quality		■			

GR 331130

OS Landranger Sheet 198

Distance: 2 miles (3½ km)

Time: 1½ - 2 hrs

Starting Point: Underhill Lane Car Park, nr. Ditchling

The village of Ditchling itself is set back away from the foot of the escarpment and an ascent from there would involve a lot of walking over the valley clay. However, by driving to the foot of the scarp, parking is to be found on the right just before the Brighton road climbs out of the valley at point GR 325137.

Begin by leaving the car park and walking east, along a small lane, signposted 'Underhill Lane, Narrow Road'. Walk down the road to the village of Westmeston, a distance of about one mile. Just immediately before the main village street is reached, turn right on a bridleway, signposted to Westmeston Bostall. This runs up through the farmyard of Westmeston Farm and then up a wooded lane to emerge onto the open hillside at the foot of the scarp. Continue on the track, which bears round to the left, and follow it until a post on the right marks a junction with a path running back right across the hillside. Follow this path through a small thicket and then up a grassy shelf as it rises across the scarp to reach the brow close to where the Brighton road crosses. Turn right, cross the road and continue up to the summit, where the trig point is found slightly to the left of the main track. Ditchling Beacon has a commanding view northwards over the Low and High Weald, although the view to the south is rather disappointing. Return to the track and turn left, shortly passing through a small gate on the right into a field. Cross straight over the small field and through another gate before turning left and following a steeply descending path, again running across the scarp and then through woods. After the wood, a wire fence is met; turn left here, up some steps and then right down through another wood on a path that leads back to the car park.

Crowborough

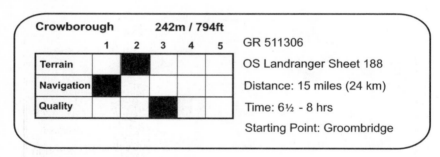

Crowborough						242m / 794ft
	1	2	3	4	5	GR 511306
Terrain		■				OS Landranger Sheet 188
Navigation	■					Distance: 15 miles (24 km)
Quality			■			Time: 6½ - 8 hrs
						Starting Point: Groombridge

You might expect the High Weald, landscape of hidden wooded valleys, sweeping heaths and thick forests, to rise to a high summit amidst a rough sandstone heath, surrounded by a girdle of woodland shrouding a host of deeply dissected valleys. Were it not for a strange quirk of geology and human history then this would be the case – Ashdown Forest, one of the south's last unspoilt heaths, would be the top. But it is not. For the real summit, it is necessary to turn to the leafy suburbs of the quiet East Sussex town of Crowborough, to what is just another residential street and the owners of one house who probably do not even realise its significance. This is the true summit of the High Weald.

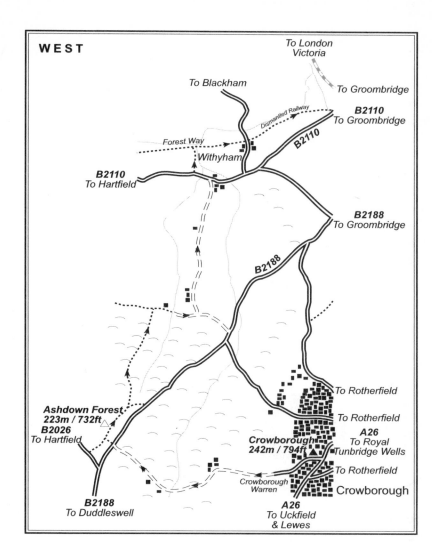

WEST

To London
Victoria

To Blackham

To Groombridge

B2110
To Groombridge

Dismantled Railway

Forest Way

B2110

Withyham

B2110
To Hartfield

B2188
To Groombridge

B2188

To Rotherfield

To Rotherfield

Ashdown Forest
223m / 732ft
B2026
To Hartfield

A26
To Royal
Tunbridge Wells

Crowborough
242m / 794ft

To Rotherfield

Crowborough
Warren

Crowborough

B2188
To Duddleswell

A26
To Uckfield
& Lewes

Getting there is not too difficult either – you can even park on the very summit – but, to see the best of the High Weald – and around Crowborough there is no shortage of excellent scenery – it is best to start further away. In fact, Groombridge is a good place, tucked away in the higher upper reaches of the Medway valley on the Kent border. There is free parking in the village, in a small car park opposite the post office, which is on the Eridge road out of the village. Although this route is quite

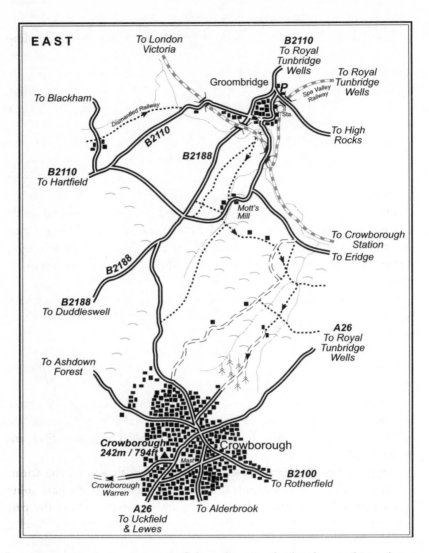

EAST

To London Victoria

To Blackham

Dismantled Railway

B2110

B2188

B2110 To Hartfield

Groombridge

B2110 To Royal Tunbridge Wells

To Royal Tunbridge Wells

Spa Valley Railway

P

Sta.

To High Rocks

Mott's Mill

To Crowborough Station

To Eridge

B2188

B2188 To Duddleswell

To Ashdown Forest

A26 To Royal Tunbridge Wells

Crowborough 242m / 794ft

Crowborough

Mast

B2100 To Rotherfield

Crowborough Warren

A26 To Uckfield & Lewes

To Alderbrook

long in comparison to many of the others in the book, anything shorter becomes a walk just confined to Crowborough; it can of course be split in half if transport can be arranged. However, in order to enjoy the fine scenery of the High Weald, it is best to walk the whole route.

The route begins almost opposite the car park, just to the right of the post office. Here, a small lane climbs gently uphill and winds through the village before dropping back down to the marshy lower ground where raised walkways have been provided to help walkers in times of flooding. There are two footpaths that take off to the right and our route takes the second one, after the pumping station. This cuts straight across the meadow to reach a tunnel underneath the Oxted to Uckfield railway line. In winter, when the water table is high, the tunnel is flooded and this part of the route is impassable.

On the far side of the railway line, the path splits. Both branches aim left and our route follows the one furthest left, which climbs up the hill and across the field to the left of the pillbox in the hillside ahead. This is also the route of the 'High Weald Landscape Trail' and, after a short distance, they both cross into another field and continue across that on the same line to a gate and stile on the edge of a wood. Through this, the path descends into the bottom of a small valley and then, passing through a further gate, climbs gently up the long and narrow field that lies in the bottom of this wooded valley.

Towards the head of the field, the path climbs to the top right-hand corner where a stile gives access to some woodland. The route continues through this, branching left at a fork and then going straight ahead at a junction at the back of some houses, to reach the small hamlet of Mott's Mill and the road once again. Following the road more or less straight ahead, it soon starts to climb the bank on the right-hand side of the valley and, after passing the last house on the right, emerges into fields. Here, paths take off to the left and right but our route takes the left-hand one, which is still waymarked as both the 'High Weald Landscape Trail' and 'Sussex Border Path'.

Dropping down the bracken-clad hillside, the path reaches the stream once again and a footbridge leads across it. On the far side, the path splits. Rather than following the valley to the right, our route follows the path that climbs half right and then left up the edge of a block of woodland to a gate at the top left corner of the field, ignoring two earlier gates on the left that give access to a pair of woodland rides in Rocks Wood. The path then slants across the next two fields before following the left-hand edge of the third to the house at Bullfinches. Here, however, the path continues its line and, after entering the head of the house's driveway, crosses a stile on the right into a sloping field. The path descends across to a gate at the bottom by a tennis court on the left. Ahead, the path continues its line, passing just to the left of the corner of the wood on the right of the field and going just to the right of a small subsequent block of woodland in the middle of the field. At the bottom, a stile leads across a footbridge to reach a small track running through the valley.

Cross straight over this and follow the path ahead, which continues along the foot of the wood on the right, before turning half right across the field when the edge of the wood turns to the right. The path now reaches a small clump of trees higher in the field, but continues along their lower edge to reach a crosspaths on the ridge above the next small valley.

Here again, the route goes straight on and, after going to the right of a hedge, enters the next field and slants downhill across it to a gateway in the bottom right-hand corner of the field in the bottom of the valley. It is now that the main ascent to Crowborough begins. A path turns to the right here but first it follows along the bottom edge of the field to the left to reach the field's left-hand edge, where it follows the stream up the valley. In due course, trees force the path and field edge uphill to the right and, when the opportunity arises to drop into the valley again, resist it and keep straight on to reach another crosspaths at a clump of trees.

Still keeping straight on, the path, now more level, continues to the top of the field before diving into another small block of woodland. On the far side of this, the path crosses a small field to reach the front of the house at Stonehouse Farm. The path crosses a stile in the driveway but then, after a few yards, leaves the drive by crossing another stile on the left before curving concentrically with the drive but running in a small overgrown paddock above the barn conversion on the left. Beyond the farm's gate, cross over another stile onto the access road where it splits to the farm and barn conversion.

The tarmac access road now begins to climb and soon enters woodland. Its ascent is intermittent but its route is obvious and the tarmac should be followed, ignoring all of the other woodland tracks, to the house at the top of the wood. Here, through a gate, the foot of the public road is found and, a little further up the hill, the edge of the town of Crowborough is reached. From here to the summit, it is an exercise of walking on pavements.

Firstly, follow this road to its end, where a left turn should be made to reach the set of traffic lights in the middle of the town at the A26. Here, turn to the right and follow this road further up the hill, until, after a stiff climb, the telecommunications mast appears on the left. Just before this, benches have been provided on either side of the road for weary walkers climbing up out of the town. Continue past the mast and raised reservoirs on the left, which some consider to be the summit, and, ignoring the road on the right opposite them, take the next turning on the right, Warren Road. Ahead, the road soon rises to its highest point at the driveway of the second house on the right – Bannockburn. The true summit lies in the garden but this is close enough for most and it is certainly not worth upsetting the owner to get any closer for the sake of a foot of height.

The route back lies over Ashdown Forest, but first there is a significant descent into another of the High Weald's secluded valleys. This begins by continuing along Warren Road, crossing the entrance of Aviemore Drive on the right and dropping further to reach a crossroads with Rannoch Drive. Keep straight ahead along Warren Road and over another crossroads where the road continues as a track along a ridge to a cluster of impressive houses at the end of the ridge. Swinging left across the front of the Clock House, a track now drops steeply into the valley on the left, across which are the huts of the Crowborough Training Camp. When close to the valley floor, the track enters the trees and continues to descend. On reaching the valley floor, swing left to cross two streams before beginning to climb again. The track now swings to the right above the Old Mill and ascends past a rather attractive house on the left all the way up to the open land of Ashdown Forest. On the ascent, there are occasional views through the trees to the dominating bulk of the South Downs.

At the road, cross straight over and pass through a small parking area to reach a broad track that marks the course of a Roman road and, more recently, the Wealdway. A right turn leads across the heath, parallel to the modern road, to the highest point, from where there are good views of the North and South Downs ahead and to the rear respectively. Soon after this, another broad track joins obliquely from the left but keep straight on and, very shortly, fork right before then forking left, still following the Wealdway waymarkers. In fact, the route follows the Wealdway all the way down into the floor of the Medway valley at Withyham.

Continuing ahead past a regenerating area of burnt heath on the left, the track forks at the edge of the wooded slopes of the forest. Aim left but this track soon curves back right and joins with another before shrinking to a small footpath that continues through the trees. The descent is broken when the path runs over a more level shoulder at mid-height before continuing the descent. In the lower wood, which the path enters through a gate, go straight over a crosstracks and continue to follow the main track and Wealdway markers down to the foot of the wood with its high deer fences.

Here, turn to the right and descend down into the bottom of another small valley past a house on the left. On the valley floor, the tarmac drive of the house is joined and a stiff climb now follows as the road climbs up out of this small valley. At the top of the slope, it swings to the left and then turns back to the right. Once around this right-hand bend, turn to the left on another track before being directed onto a footpath ahead. This recent path diversion takes walkers around below the large manor house above Withyham. It then rejoins the access road by some more impressive buildings and follows it gradually downhill to Withyham. When the road forks by the church, aim left to complete the descent down to the Hartfield to Groombridge road.

A left turn on this road leads across a small tributary of the Medway before the Wealdway turns off to the right. Follow this half left across the first field and then ahead across the second to a gate at the far side. Here, the Wealdway crosses the old East Grinstead to Tunbridge Wells railway line. Now joining the Forest Way, our route turns to the right and follows the old railway trackbed. Its level and straight course and good surface make for a quick if unexciting return along the valley towards Groombridge. First, a road is crossed at the old Withyham station but the line continues along the valley, through a cutting, under a bridge and onto an embankment. On this embankment, the track drops down to the right and continues along the foot of the slope to the end of the trail and onto the main road once again. From now on, it is a simple enough stroll back into Groombridge. Following the road to the left, it crosses over the existing railway line and then runs through the outskirts of the village to bend sharp left where the Crowborough road goes off to the right. Here, aim more or less straight on along a gravel track that cuts across to the road along which the day's walk was first started. When this road is met, following it ahead and around leads back through the village to the post office and car park.

Chanctonbury Hill

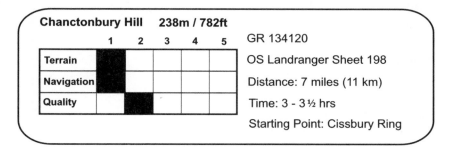

Chanctonbury Hill	238m / 782ft					
	1	2	3	4	5	GR 134120
Terrain	■					OS Landranger Sheet 198
Navigation	■					Distance: 7 miles (11 km)
Quality		■				Time: 3 - 3 ½ hrs
						Starting Point: Cissbury Ring

Chanctonbury Hill is the highest point of the South Downs between the Rivers Arun and Adur. The hill can be climbed from all sides although, in this case, vehicular access to the ridge itself is not possible. The best approach is up the dipslope from Cissbury Ring near Findon.

The approach to the car park at Cissbury Ring is far from obvious. The village of Findon lies next to the A24 and can be reached from the A24/A280 roundabout. Following the road down from the A24, a crossroads is reached. Keep straight on here and follow the road ahead straight up the hill ignoring any other turnings on both the right and left. At the top of the village, where the road swings to the right, turn left on a small surfaced lane that leads all the way up to the car park just below the hill fort.

The walk begins by turning away from the Ring and following a broad, sometimes greasy track straight ahead as far as a 'triangle' junction at a small thicket. Turn left here but soon leave this track for a small path that takes off to the right. This path now maintains a fairly level course as far as a junction at which a right turn should be made. The main descent now follows as the path leads down a leafy lane to a house. Following its driveway onwards, a gateway on the right, opposite where another track joins on the left, is found. Turn right through the gate and cross over the field to another gate through which the road in the valley bottom is reached.

A rusty gate almost opposite marks the route onwards through another paddock to reach a track on the far side. Turn left here and follow the track, which now climbs quite steeply uphill to reach a crosstracks on the ridge. Turning to the right, a slow steady climb ensues all the way to the summit, ignoring any track deviating to the right or left. The first object found is a dewpond up on the left just before a cattle grid. Once over the

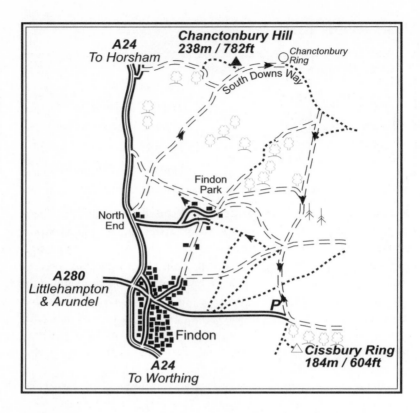

grid, the trig point cannot be seen but aim half left across the grass and it is soon reached at which point the fine northwards view ahead unfolds. Continuing along the ridge, the track leads onwards to the old hill fort which is now a fenced thicket and on along the ridge to a prominent crosstracks.

A right turn here gradually leads back down another ridge. A track soon joins on the left and then, further on, another joins acutely from the right. At the next junction bear half left and the outwards route is rejoined about a mile from the car park. Those who still have energy to spare are advised to cross straight over the road and climb up to the hill fort of Cissbury Ring with its prominent earthworks and flint mines.

Firle Beacon

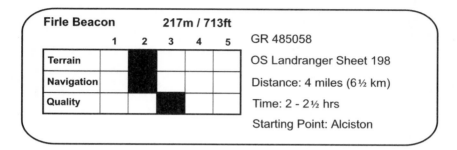

Firle Beacon			217m / 713ft			
	1	2	3	4	5	
Terrain		■				
Navigation		■				
Quality			■			

GR 485058

OS Landranger Sheet 198

Distance: 4 miles (6 ½ km)

Time: 2 - 2 ½ hrs

Starting Point: Alciston

Alciston is a pretty little village up a dead-end street off the A27 between Eastbourne and Lewes. Park on the village street, as high up as is possible and then walk to the end of the tarmac and then up a tree-lined track to meet another track running from left to right. Turn right and soon a path runs left up the edge of a field. Follow this initially up the headland and then through a sunken lane on the left until it meets another path at the foot of the scarp. Walk left a few yards and then right up a path which runs left across the face of the scarp. It reaches the ridge at a stile, a short distance beyond which is the South Downs Way. Turn right and follow it to the car park at Bopeep Bostall. Keep straight on and up the hill opposite and then along before rising up again, this time to the summit and trig point slightly to the right of the path. The summit commands fine seaward views of Newhaven to the south and also of the Weald to the north.

Reverse the ascent down the first small hill and then, when it levels off, turn half left and cross to the fence running along the top of the scarp and follow it until a gate gives access to a path running back obliquely down

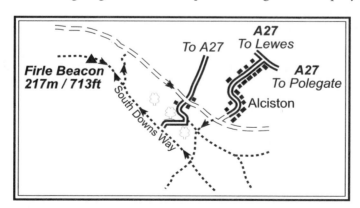

the hillside. Go down this path and then walk down a wooded path to emerge at a crosstracks. Turn right, pass Upper Barn and a cottage on the left, cross the road and continue down the track through the converted buildings of Bopeep Farm to rejoin the route of ascent just above Alciston.

Wilmington Hill

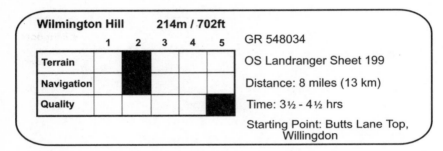

Wilmington Hill	214m / 702ft					
	1	2	3	4	5	GR 548034
Terrain		■				OS Landranger Sheet 199
Navigation		■				Distance: 8 miles (13 km)
Quality					■	Time: 3½ - 4½ hrs
						Starting Point: Butts Lane Top, Willingdon

Wilmington Hill is the easternmost separate summit of the South Downs and the highest point of the block of high ground that falls away to the sea at Beachy Head. However, an approach from this direction is long and does not show the northern escarpment – the hill's best feature – at all. Thus, the most convenient place to park is on the downs above the village of Willingdon, just off the A22 between Polegate and Eastbourne.

To reach the car park, leave the A22 to enter a side loop that runs through the village of Willingdon. From the north, this turn is unsignposted but, after the turn off to the cemetery, there is a crossroads at a set of traffic lights and the required turn is on the right a short distance beyond. When the road reaches the old village, it begins to bend and, before reaching the centre, turn right again up a steeply rising road; the car park is at its end. From Eastbourne, the turn is signposted to Willingdon Village and is a short distance in advance of the roundabout where the A2021 road from the other end of the town meets the A22.

Our route starts off by following one of the northwards tracks along the ridge, which join whilst traversing the western slopes of the first small summit, Cold Crouch. Just beyond, a junction of paths is reached where a path climbs up from Willingdon on the right. Here, the Wealdway goes

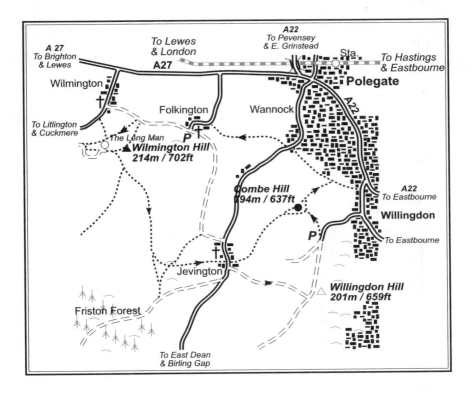

left and a further path climbs half left to the top of the next hill. However, our route keeps straight on towards a waymarker on an initially indistinct path that is also the 1066 Country Walk. This makes a descending traverse around the head of the steep valley of Tas Combe on the right, before reaching the ridge descending north-eastwards from the top of the hill at a signposted junction.

At this point, keep straight on along the Willingdon Path. This cuts through a scrubby hedge, before descending across a steep bank (ignore the level sheeptracks running along the hillside). At the foot of the slope, a lower path is met that runs just above the field fence. A right turn on this then leads, above a small wood, to the head of a short flight of steps on the left. At the foot of these, the path leads down the left-hand side of a field to meet a path running along the very foot of the slope just behind the village.

There now follows a walk along the foot of the hillside to beyond the Long Man at Wilmington, from where the final ascent commences. To begin with, this path is followed to the left, above the cemetery, and then across a public field, before running straight ahead out to the road at Wannock. The onwards route now continues to the small village of Folkington, so first follow this road to the left. After a first road is passed on the right and then a large house with an ornamental duck pond, a broad track runs to the right beyond the last house and into the field behind. When in the field, the track swings slowly around to the left before turning back right to cross a stream. Once over the stream, it turns sharply back left and continues up until another track turns off across the field to the right. This then leads to a concrete farm road atop the ridge ahead, over which a gate allows access to a steeply descending path inside a wood; another field is then crossed to reach the small lane leading to the village.

The village is now not far to the left and this route follows the road all the way to its end at a small car parking area in the copse beyond the church. Here, the Wealdway is met, running from left to right. To the right, it leads along, gently ascending up the edge of the wood with fields on the right. Ignoring a gate on the left in an open stretch, the path enters the next copse before forking. Keep going along the hillside and take the left fork in preference to the descending right branch. Now on the open face of Wilmington Hill, the path takes a fairly level course along to the foot of the chalk-carved figure of Long Man on the slope; a little further on, through a gate, a crosstracks is reached.

Now the ascent up to Wilmington Hill begins up this track to the left. This soon merges with the South Downs Way, which joins from the right above the hollow of Ewe Dean on the far side of the ridge. Not far beyond that, the main track swings to the right to make a circuitous ascent, but it is much more preferable to stay by the fence on the left on a narrow path that passes above the Long Man to rejoin the South Downs Way on the top of this shoulder. However, once the South Downs Way is rejoined, still stay on the grass by the fence on the left and continue along there and through a gate to the trig point and tumulus that mark the summit on the edge of the northern escarpment.

The view from here is superb. The coastline is seen to stretch in a virtually unbroken line from the other side of Hastings through Eastbourne and Cuckmere to Brighton and beyond. Inland, the patchwork landscape of the Low Weald rises slowly into the more wooded slopes of the High Weald on the northern skyline, whilst the Isle of Wight is just visible on clear days to the south-west. However, it is the fine scarp scenery of Firle Beacon and the rest of the South Downs that steals the scene, stretching away eastwards in a seemingly unbroken whaleback.

The return to the starting point involves a descent down to Jevington, the birthplace of Banoffie Pie, and then a sizeable reascent back to the car park. For most of this part of the route, the South Downs Way is kept underfoot and this is reached initially by backtracking the short distance to the last gate. Here, a left turn on the far side of the fence leads down and around the corner until the waymarked route across the upland pastures appears not far to the right. This track then swings to the right and descends a ridge above Jevington Holt on the left. Soon, after entering the valley's wooded upper slopes, the route turns left and descends steeply to the foot of the wood before reaching a fork after a more level section. Go right here and continue to drop down, now by fields, to the church in Jevington; a small lane then leads down to the village street here.

The tearoom is now more or less opposite and the South Downs Way turns to the right here and, very shortly, takes the second lane on the left, running up the far side of the tearoom. After passing a farm entrance on the left, this turns into a rough track that climbs, initially up a green sunken lane, to the summit of Willingdon Hill. Just before the trig point and true summit is reached and, unless the true summit is to be gained, a left turn here leads back to the car park, bypassing the masts on the wooded top of Babylon Down.

Castle Hill

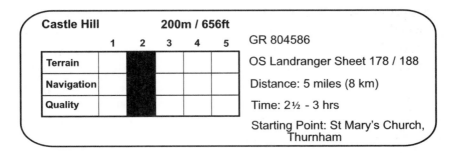

Castle Hill		200m / 656ft			
	1	2	3	4	5
Terrain		■			
Navigation		■			
Quality		■			

GR 804586

OS Landranger Sheet 178 / 188

Distance: 5 miles (8 km)

Time: 2½ - 3 hrs

Starting Point: St Mary's Church, Thurnham

Castle Hill is the middle summit of the three in the North Downs and certainly the most insignificant. It lies just to the east of Maidstone, just

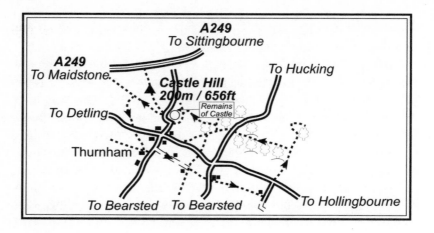

above the village of Bearsted, overlooking Leeds Castle on the foot of the greensand slopes on the opposite side of the intervening valley, which is home to the M20 and the new Channel Tunnel Rail Link.

The best place to start a circular walk on the hill is the small village of Thurnham, which lies at the foot of the escarpment on the Maidstone side of the ridge. It can be reached up a road from Bearsted Station. There is good roadside parking on the left by the pathway leading to St Mary's Church before the village crossroads is reached. Alternatively, Thurnham can be reached from the A249 dual carriageway through the village of Detling. A right turn in Thurnham at the crossroads by the Black Horse Inn then leads down a small hill to the parking on the right.

Just slightly uphill of the entrance to the church, and on the opposite side of the road, a private tarmac roadway takes off to the right. This runs below various houses to reach the oast-houses at the end of the lane, now a private residence. Keeping straight on, the right of way passes through a gate to the front of another house and then crosses a stile onto the top of the field beyond. The path then follows this headland out to another road leading up from Bearsted opposite the riding centre at Cobham Manor.

Somewhat down the road to the right, a footpath sign on the opposite side points into a driveway and the frontage of a house. The right of way passes this on its right and then crosses a stile into the paddock beyond. Here, it follows the left-hand edge before crossing a stile into the next field and passing out of that through a gate to a trackway. Down to the left, and still part of the riding centre, is a small show-jumping arena but our route goes ahead and up some steps opposite.

A stile at the top of these steps then leads into the next paddock and a stile at the far right corner again gives access to the next where the path slants half left to the next. These paddocks are still all part of the riding centre's estate and, over this small transverse trackway, the path crosses another stile into the next field and follows the right-hand edge of that to the far side. Beyond this, the path then keeps straight on over two more stiles and down alongside a hedge to a gate into a garden.

The occupiers of this house would clearly prefer walkers to use the unofficial path to the right around the outside of the garden. However, the right of way runs through the garden and it is not as difficult as is inferred by the notice. The gate ahead gives access to a path that runs along the top of the lawn, separated from the house on the left by a hedge and passes out into the roadway on the far side through a gate between trees.

Now the ascent up onto the downs begins and, initially, this follows the road up to the left to meet the other road that has been running along the foot of the scarp from Detling through Thurnham to Hollingbourne. Our route crosses straight over and climbs up the gradually rising path on the far side. This climbs towards the ridge but, when a stile is reached on the left, it should be crossed. Now, the North Downs Way is underfoot and that is followed almost all the way to the summit, although there are some steep ups and downs before then.

To begin with, the path climbs steeply uphill, to cross another stile at the top of this field and run inside the wooded top of the escarpment, before then descending steeply to meet Coldblow Lane, running from the riding stables down on the left to Stockbury on the right. However, our route crosses straight over and follows the gently ascending track opposite, still amongst the trees. This curves around the hillside before the waymarked route of the North Downs Way drops back down some steps on the left to the bottom of the wood.

The descent is short-lived, however, since the path immediately begins to climb steeply up steps once again to reach the next hilltop. A gradual descent then follows before the path leaves the wood over a stile into the bottom of a field. The wooded knoll over the next small valley is the shoulder of the hill that contains the earthworks of the old castle and the North Downs Way makes its way to the foot of the hill by following the fence around the head of this small valley and then dropping back down on the far side to meet the road climbing up from Thurnham on the left.

The crossroads by the Black Horse is only a quarter of a mile down to the left and, obviously, if preferred, this first section of the walk could be omitted in favour of a short walk up the road to this point. However, the walk now continues by following this road up the hill to the right. After curving around below the castle on the right, the North Downs Way branches left over the next stile and, here, it should be left in order to climb the final slopes to the summit of Castle Hill.

Instead of turning left over the stile, the summit path slants half left over the unfenced field above. Once over the immediate skyline, the trig point comes into view ahead, a little to the left of some trees and a house that are now on the horizon. The trig point does not actually mark the true summit and some parts of the field are a few feet higher. However, it is left for readers to determine the true and nondescript summit and then decide whether they wish to reach it, of course being careful not to damage the crop at all.

The descent back to the village is much shorter and begins by returning to the road by the castle. Now, follow the North Downs Way to the right over a stile; the path continues along below the fence until that turns right, at which point the path keeps on and over a small valley, passing two lone trees en route. On the top of the next ridge, an old waymaker post is found in a solitary bush, together with the remnants of the old fence. Here, the route turns left, leaving the North Downs Way, and crosses over a stile at the bottom of the slope, half left across the next field and out to the road over a further stile.

The church at Thurnham is now in view half left and the path goes towards it across the stile opposite, again running half left across the next field. The path reaches a hedge on the left of the field, in which a stile gives access to a small lane. On the opposite side of this private road, a gate leads into the churchyard, which the path crosses and then runs out to the road by the car parking area.

Cheriton Hill

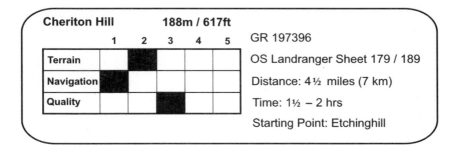

Cheriton Hill	188m / 617ft				
	1	2	3	4	5
Terrain		■			
Navigation	■				
Quality			■		

GR 197396

OS Landranger Sheet 179 / 189

Distance: 4½ miles (7 km)

Time: 1½ – 2 hrs

Starting Point: Etchinghill

Cheriton is the most easterly of the hills on the North Downs and stands as the highest point of the downland plateau above Hythe, Folkestone and its suburb of Cheriton, where the Channel Tunnel begins. With the construction of the tunnel terminal, industry now laps onto the hill's southern slopes above Cheriton and so it is from the west, from the small village of Etchinghill, that the most pleasing ascent may be made. Although at first glance it may appear that the route contains much roadwalking, these lanes are so narrow, grown-in and infrequently used that they are more like farm tracks than roads.

In the village of Etchinghill, opportunities for car parking are relatively few. The best place would appear to be on the left-hand side of the Hawkinge road out of the village – Teddars Lee Road – on the perimeter of the golf course. However, patrons of the New Inn may be able, with permission, to leave their cars in its substantial car park.

The route begins by heading south on the Hythe road out of the village before slanting off to the left down a small lane at the end of the village. This is actually the driveway to Coombe Farm but the North Downs Way and our route soon escapes over a stile on the left. The path then cuts across the first field, aiming for the far right corner, from where it continues through woods and passes underneath the disused Elham valley railway line. After crossing a short field, the path reaches the scarp foot and turns to follow it half right along the bottom of a field.

After curving around the corner, the path and field enter a small combe where the field opens out. Our route then ascends all the way up the floor of this steep valley to its head at the top of the scarp slope, continuing to follow the North Downs Way waymarkers. Once at the top, the path turns

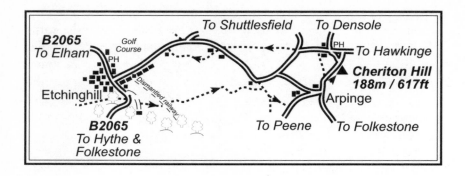

sharply back to the right before turning to the left with the fence. Once across a stile and into the next field, the path turns sharply to the left again and follows the fence around to the right in due course to a further stile. The path then follows the boundary on the left over this field to reach a stile into a green lane at the far side.

Here, the route turns to the right and continues until, after only a short distance, there is a somewhat dilapidated stile on the left. Now leaving the North Downs Way, a path cuts across this field, following the line of the telegraph poles to another fairly ruinous stile by a gate at the far side. One more field, which is crossed to a final grown-in stile by following the right-hand fence, remains before a small lane is reached just below Arpinge. A left turn leads up into the hamlet and a junction of lanes.

A right and then a left leads up another lane that gently climbs the hill's upper slopes to reach its summit at an open gateway on the right, not far from a communications mast further to the right, although the summit is reached before the mast's access track. The trig point beyond the mast is, however, at a lower elevation. On a clear day the view from the summit is quite extensive. The broad curve of the coastline beyond Hythe can be seen to continue along the shingle spit to the nuclear power station at Dungeness. Meanwhile, beyond the near shoreline at Sandgate, the broad expanse of the Channel separates Kent from the distant silhouette of the French coast.

The descent back to Etchinghill is not dissimilar to the ascent and it begins by following the lane onwards and then around to the left at a junction. This leads to a further junction by the Cat Inn at Paddlesworth, where a left turn leads down a slightly sunken lane to a further road junction. Here, a path opposite makes a gentle ascent over a further piece of high ground, cutting a straight line across three fields to reach the scarp-top road in the vicinity of Shearins Farm. Again almost opposite, another path begins and this runs straight across a first paddock to a stile into a larger field. In this second field, turn to the right and just cut across the corner to a ruinous stile with the crosspiece missing. From here, the path cuts through a shelter-belt to reach another horse paddock, which the path leaves by means of another stile in the bottom far corner.

Once over this stile, the route has reached the edge of another steep-sided combe. A descent into it is, however, avoided by means of following a slanting shelf around its head and then walking along the top of the slope on the far side until a stile, which is easily missed, gives access to a field on the right. The path then crosses this, aiming just to the right of the black and white house at the far side to reach the Hawkinge road out of Etchinghill. The village is now only a short stroll to the left.

Cliffe Hill

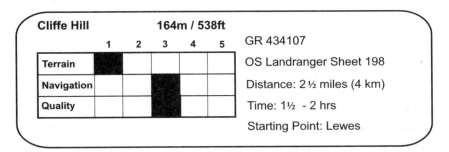

Cliffe Hill		164m / 538ft			
	1	2	3	4	5
Terrain	■				
Navigation			■		
Quality			■		

GR 434107

OS Landranger Sheet 198

Distance: 2 ½ miles (4 km)

Time: 1½ - 2 hrs

Starting Point: Lewes

Cliffe Hill, in many ways, is proof of the value of the concept of relative height. Although only 538 feet high, it rises from just about sea level on all sides and takes just as much effort to climb as any other higher hill in the area.

Park just out of Lewes on the A26 London road on the right, in a small lay-by just after an Esso garage on the left. Walk away from Lewes a short distance up the pavement until some tiny steps on the right lead up from the pavement and then a path leads along the edge of a wood, over a small green, to what looks like a dead-end. However, when a brown wooden

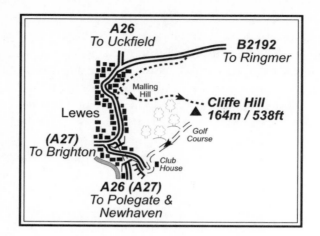

fence is shortly reached, the path runs around the back and to the right of it, small and narrow but quite clear. Follow this path (which may be difficult with a very large rucksack) up behind the fence until a stile, missing a through-plank, on the right, leads out of the wood and onto a patch of what looks like wasteground.

From here things quickly improve; a track, leading rightwards, ascends across the hill, soon turning to the left and running above the nature reserve of Malling Down. After the second gate it enters the reserve and becomes a path. Ignore a stile on the left and continue around the head of the valley until, just before the path enters a thicket, a dilapidated stile on the left gives access onto Lewes Golf Course. Walk up the right-hand side on the edge of the wood, around the head of a green, and then up the right-hand side of an old hedgerow to reach the trig point, which has now appeared into view.

Avoiding flying golf balls on the fairway, walk in a south-west direction, aiming for a black and white striped marker post, beyond which is a track leading down through the woods. Follow the track downhill, past the maintenance shed on the right, over a crosstracks and down through trees along the edge of the course before emerging and continuing on the same line. Shortly, it bends to the left and runs above an obelisk to arrive at the clubhouse. Follow the drive down into the town, taking a peep at some point over the massive chalk cliffs immediately to the left (care required!) to follow down through the quaint old houses of Chapel Hill to reach Lewes itself. Turn right at the crossroads and follow the road to the left and then to the right to reach the A26 at a roundabout. Turn right and cross at a pedestrian crossing. Pass a roundabout and entrance to Cuilfail Tunnel on the right before crossing back over the road at a pedestrian refuge in the middle and continuing up the pavement to the small lay-by in which the car is parked.

Section 5 – The Cotswolds

The River Avon from the Bristol Channel to Malmesbury. The clay vale from there to Swindon and the Vale of the White Horse to Abingdon. The Thames from there to Wallingford and the foot of the chalk escarpment to Luton. The Grand Union Canal and then the foot of the stone belt scarp to Tewkesbury. The River Severn from there to Avonmouth.

NAME	HEIGHT	IN SECTION	IN ENGLAND	IN BRITAIN
Cleeve Hill	330m / 1083ft	01 of 02	123 of 184	1324J of 1552
Bredon Hill	299m / 980ft	02 of 02	137 of 184	1373 of 1552

Picturesque honey-stone villages, babbling brooks and a wide, open upland area are all images of the Cotswolds. Quaint villages like Bourton-on-the-Water, Charlbury and Lechlade stand alongside sturdy and substantial towns of big square-cut stone, such as Chipping Norton, Moreton-in-Marsh and Stow-on-the-Wold. To the south and east the ground dips gently away into clay vales and, to the north, a stone ridge continues through Nottinghamshire into Lincolnshire and Yorkshire (Volumes 2 and 3). To the west, however, the ground falls sharply and steeply away over a curving escarpment to the fertile loamy soils of the fruit-growing and market garden country of the Vale of Evesham.

The Cotswolds form one of the most famous parts of a long stone ridge that runs from the Dorset coast (Section 3) all the way to the North Yorkshire Moors (Vol 3). This ridge is formed entirely from a succession of Jurassic age rocks, all deposited around 190 million years ago. At this time, Britain was experiencing changing marine conditions in its position at the edge of a large ocean and this is reflected in the rock types then deposited.

At the end of the Triassic period, the harsh deserts, which had prevailed for many millions of years, disappeared as a shallow ocean began to spread across Britain. Some highland areas, such as the Mendips (Section 2)

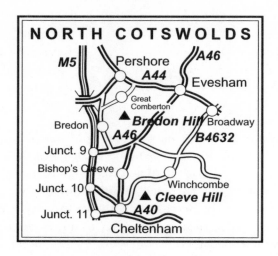

escaped this transgression and instead remained as islands surrounded by an ocean rich in ammonites and large marine reptiles, such as the Plesiosaur. During this time, successive layers of thin limestones and clays were deposited in a sequence called the Lias. These rocks form the foundation of the Cotswolds and make up the soils of the Vale of Evesham. In places, rich bacterial colonies created iron compounds that gave an ochre colour to the rocks. The resulting ironstones are more common in the central part of the stone ridge and are responsible for the red soils and rocks of the Banbury area.

As the Jurassic continued, an uplift of the central part of the North Sea led to the development of estuaries and deltas further north. However, in the Cotswolds, the sea shallowed and calcium carbonate precipitated out of the water to form tiny nodules or ooliths on the ocean floor. This has given rise to the grainy texture of the Cotswold limestones. The first limestone band that was deposited is the Inferior Oolite and it is this stone that is used in many of the Cotswold villages. It is separated from the Great Oolite above it, which forms the famous Bath stone, by a thin layer of clay formed from volcanic ash, known as Fuller's earth (see Section 4).

Again, these limestones contain periodic concentrations of iron, which provide a variety of colours in the Cotswold stone from the classic yellow, through the honey colours of the Bath stone towards other russet-coloured stones. The Great Oolite was followed by a marked change in deposition towards thick clays and limestones, which heralded the onset of the late

Jurassic. Marine conditions once more became dominant over all Britain and a thick band of Oxford Clay was deposited, followed by the Corallian limestone and the Kimmeridge Clay. However, during the late Jurassic, the ocean began to retreat southwards and as a result the last rocks to be deposited in the Jurassic sequence – the Portland and Purbeck limestones – are to be found only on the Dorset coast (Section 3).

As discussed in Section 3, the late Cretaceous saw a shallow sea cover Britain to deposit a thick layer of chalk before the subsidence of the North Sea basin and the opening of the Atlantic Ocean saw a doming of northern and western Britain and a dipping of the south and east. Erosion then proceeded to wear away the chalk from much of Britain, including the Cotswolds, leaving the northern chalk scarp to run along from Luton past Goring to Swindon and Yeovil.

Similar weathering also affected the stone belt to form a parallel scarp slope running from Warwickshire through Banbury and Cheltenham to Chipping Sodbury and Lyme Regis. Towards the foot of the south-eastern-facing dipslope, the mid-Jurassic oolitic limestones disappear below the late Jurassic Oxford Clay where the clay has not been eroded altogether. This, the first of two clay vales, supports the waters of the infant River Thames as far as Oxford. This vale is then superseded by a miniature scarp formed from the upper Jurassic Corallian limestone, which the Thames breaks through at Oxford. Thick clay soils, this time the Kimmeridge Clay, then once again dominate across a second broad vale, known between Abingdon and Swindon as the Vale of the White Horse, before the ground rises sharply at the foot of the chalk escarpment (Section 3).

Any traveller going westwards along the M4 is well rewarded with an excellent opportunity to study the relief of the scarplands. From Reading, the motorway climbs up out of the syncline of the London Basin (Section 4) to reach its highest point on the chalklands (Section 3) near Membury service station. From there a steep descent leads down the double scarp and onto the clay at Swindon before a gradual rise up the dipslope onto the stone ridge to reach its crest at Junction 18 near Chipping Sodbury. At the foot of the stone-belt scarp the motorway reaches the Lias foundation of the stone-belt, which then continues to the Bristol Channel.

Owing to the joints and bedding planes of limestones, most rainwater that falls on the surface quickly disappears underground to appear as springs either at the foot of or at mid-height on the scarp slope. This water makes the underlying Lias clays unstable, causing landslips under the weight of the heavy oolitic limestones above. This steepens the scarp slope and, over time, causes it to retreat. However, some larger blocks, such as Dundry Down at Bristol (Section 2) and Bredon Hill remained intact and formed their own scarps as the main slope retreated back leaving them isolated as impressive monoliths.

Thus the Cotswolds came into being as an upland plateau bounded on its north-western sides by a steep scarp, dipping gradually south-eastwards into thick sticky clays, with settlements like Chipping Sodbury, Wotton-under-Edge and Broadway nestling at its foot. The highest point is attained at Cleeve Hill and this forms the only separate summit of this vast tableland, whilst Bredon Hill stands alone, distant from the main scarp, looking out over the Severn valley to the Malvern Hills beyond.

Accommodation

The Cotswold area provides ample accommodation for tourists, although for the purposes of this book the towns of Cheltenham and Winchcombe would be good bases. However, there is little shortage of accommodation elsewhere from the larger towns to the small attractive villages and farms that lie along the springline in the valleys. There are youth hostels at The Ridgeway (near Wantage), Oxford, Duntisbourne, Stow-on-the-Wold and Charlbury.

Cleeve Hill

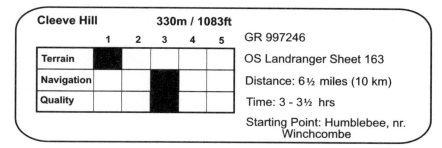

Cleeve Hill	1	2	3	4	5	330m / 1083ft
Terrain	■					
Navigation			■			
Quality			■			

GR 997246

OS Landranger Sheet 163

Distance: 6½ miles (10 km)

Time: 3 - 3½ hrs

Starting Point: Humblebee, nr. Winchcombe

Cleeve Hill is the highest point in the Cotswold Hills and rises steeply up behind the towns of Bishop's Cleeve and Cheltenham. However, it is on the Winchcombe slopes that there are the most points of interest, away from the urban sprawl.

Humblebee is the name given to a piece of woodland on the minor road between Winchcombe and Brockhampton. A small lay-by, mainly used by visitors walking to the long barrow of Bellas Knap, can be found at GR 021262 and is marked on the OS Landranger Sheet for the area.

Leave the car park by walking north-west down the road a short distance towards Winchcombe until it bends to the right. Ahead a small stile gives access to a field, signposted 'Postlip', and another stile on the left crosses a small fence and leads into a field. Aim half right and once over a small lip, a stile will be seen ahead below a small stable which gives access to the drive leading down from Corndean Hall. Walk to the right, ignoring a track leading to some buildings, and past a specimen beech tree on the left to find another stile leading into the field ahead. Walk ahead across the field aiming for what looks like a bridge but is in fact only a piece of wood in the trees. Cross the small depression above a spring and climb the slope ahead towards some steps that lead to a stile on the right. Over the stile, contour around the hill on a grassy shelf until below a thicket where, once through a hedgerow, a right turn should be made down the hill, turning left across the field when a track joins from the right, aiming for Corndean Farm.

Pass to the right of the farm and down its drive, through the buildings at Postlip Mill and up the drive to reach the main Cheltenham to Winchcombe road. Turn left and soon, when the road bends to the right, follow a track straight ahead which leads up through woods to reach the

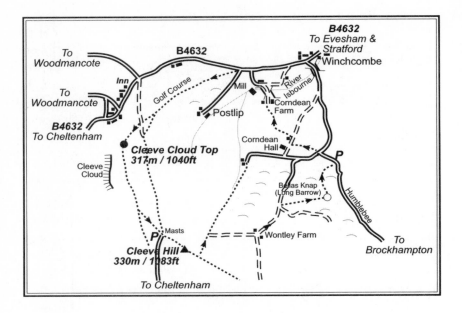

open hill. Keep going up and follow a rising cart track by the wall, which then leads across a large golf course. By the tenth tee, on the right, turn right and in a few yards the trig point on the lower northern summit, Cleeve Cloud Top, is reached. Although lower, being perched on the edge of the scarp means that this summit has the far superior views and a toposcope is to be found close by which identifies all the main features.

Continue south across the golf course and along the edge of the limestone cliffs on the right, known as Cleeve Cloud, before taking off half left over the golf course, aiming for some prominent masts ahead. Pass by the masts and follow the wall along to reach another trig point, this time marking the true summit.

Continue on a short distance, passing a large thicket of gorse bushes immediately on the left and then turn left down the edge of a wall. Soon a gate on the right gives access to a track (the Cotswold Way) that leads across open fields to the ruined buildings at Wontley Farm. Turn left here, following a dirt track until a signpost on the right points the way down the edge of a field to Humblebee and Bellas Knap Long Barrow. Taking this path, the long barrow, built in 2500 BC is soon reached. The barrow yielded the remains of 38 people buried here in four chambers, although the imposing northern entrance is false, a hoax intended to mislead hopeful grave robbers. Leaving the enclosure by the noticeboard at the back left corner, turn left on a path which runs along the edge of the wood before passing right through a gate and running downhill by a hedgerow on the right. Although the Cotswold Way leaves by a gate in the right-hand corner, the car park is best reached by leaving the field through a gate, approached by following the path that curves around the bottom headland, beyond which a path descends the short distance back to the lay-by.

Bredon Hill

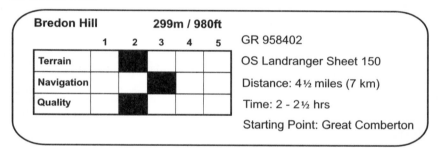

Bredon Hill		299m / 980ft				
	1	2	3	4	5	GR 958402
Terrain		■				OS Landranger Sheet 150
Navigation			■			Distance: 4½ miles (7 km)
Quality		■				Time: 2 - 2½ hrs
						Starting Point: Great Comberton

Unlike many of the other hills, Bredon Hill is not simply the highest point of a huge stretch of downland; instead it rises out of the surrounding landscape like a huge monolith, although it is composed of the same limestone as the nearby Cotswolds. Its most interesting aspect is to the north, where complicated concave slopes fall from the summit, meaning that the objective can always be clearly seen ahead.

Park at Great Comberton, easily reached from Eckington or Pershore. Although not overrun with parking spaces, there are one or two places where a car can be left on the main street. Leave the main street by a track signposted 'public footpath', which leads through the churchyard to join a smaller back street. Turn right and take the second footpath on the left, which runs along the top of a field before shortly turning into farm buildings. Walk straight through the farm and cross a stile leading into the field ahead. Follow the cart track, which leads over the field and then through two gates. Ignoring a stile on the right, keep straight on, passing through another gate and walking up a small valley to the right

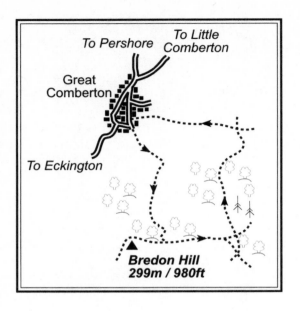

of a large knoll to reach a pair of gates in the far corner. Pass through the left-hand gate and keep by the fence on the right until a dewpond is reached on the left. Now bear half left through a small thicket to reach a track crossing from right to left. Continue following the fence uphill (which has now turned in slightly) until the final steep scarp slope is reached. Follow a path on the left, which makes a rising traverse to the left to reach the wall on the crest a short distance to the right of a crossing point. Walk back to the right once over the wall, into the hill fort and cross towards the high point at the ugly tower ahead passing a stone bearing a Ramblers' Association plaque with the view marked out on it.

Return to the wall and follow it along to the right, passing through two gates below a wood, to bear half left where the fence (now on the right) turns slightly to the right. This track leads down to below another much larger wood, where a sharp left turn should be made on a track which runs downhill, passing to the left of yet another wood. Cross straight over the field ahead and follow a muddy path steeply down through the wood ahead to reach a farm track, now out of the wood, in the valley below. Walk down this track, passing a path on the right, before turning left over a hidden bridge and stile on the left in the hedge. Turn half right and cross the field ahead, aiming for another bridge and stile slightly to the left of an open, but impassable, gateway, then continue on along the hedgerow crossing more stiles, bridges and gates to emerge on the back lane by the churchyard. A short walk back through the churchyard leads to the main road in the village.

Epilogue

It was a cold and showery winter's afternoon on the Hampshire Downs and the semi-industrial landscape of the Kennet Valley stretched away from my feet towards the distant towns of Newbury and Reading. I had visited Walbury Hill before but it was on this bracing day that the first pages of this book were written. Walbury Hill is the highest point of the Wessex Downs (Section 3) and is the nearest separate hill to my home to the west of the town of Reading.

From this distinguished summit, home to one of the largest hill forts in southern England, the sun began to set over the distant silhouette of the South Downs (Section 4). It may not have been a particularly auspicious start but it led inexorably to the day, 21 months later, when I would write the final pages of this volume after climbing Cheriton Hill on the North Downs above Folkestone (Section 4), having been frustrated by months of footpath closures due to the tragic foot-and-mouth disease outbreak.

During these 21 months, I climbed the 35 hills in this book together with many from volumes two and three as well. I saw the landscape of southern England in all four seasons, in all of its moods and in almost all weathers. I returned to many hills I had climbed before, such as Walbury Hill, and found fantastic views and aspects of hills that I never knew existed. That is the best thing about a book such as this – by climbing to all the summits, the walker can see all the landscapes of an area and then return to and explore those that particularly capture the heart. For me it was the Greensand Ridge: after climbing Black Down and Leith Hill, I was driven to explore it in great detail to find possibly my favourite view of all from Holmbury Hill (a satellite of Leith Hill, Section 4).

There are some moments that stand out and views and experiences that will stay with me for the rest of my life. A beautiful winter sunrise over the High Weald from Black Down (Section 4), as depicted in one of the book's photographs. Dodging the flying golf balls on Cliffe Hill above Lewes and of course the day I climbed Leith Hill, the highest point in south-east England, and saw the fantastic views and scenes of the Greensand Ridge for the very first time are certainly memorable.

The memory of the Hardown Hill route (Section 3) will not leave me quickly either. Sitting on the clifftop of its satellite Golden Cap on a hot and sunny summer's day and watching boats cruise around Lyme Regis and Charmouth while eating my egg and bacon sandwiches was an unforgettable scene. It is days like these that compensate for all those days in the wind and rain on the higher hills and mountains. Who says the lower hills are second-rate?

Well, I am afraid I cannot say that plodding around the tarmac roads around Staple Hill (Section 2) was all that wonderful on a cloudy cold day and trudging through the deep mud and rough fields of Dundry Down (Section 2) was not all that easy either. But the views more than made up for that. Then of course there is the Dunkery Beacon route (Section 2), my favourite walk in the book. How could anything beat that fantastic combination of sea views from the clifftop summit of Selworthy Beacon, the hidden heaths on the summit of Periton Hill, a magnificent panorama from the highest point of Exmoor – Dunkery Beacon – and an enchanting valley complete with gorges and a tumbling stream for the descent? It gets even better when there is a cream tea waiting at the foot of the hill!

That was the start of a week in Devon and Cornwall when perhaps unsurprisingly the black beast of Bodmin Moor failed to materialise and I stood amidst the white lunar landscape of Hensbarrow Beacon (Section 1). Whatever anybody else may say, I must admit that I actually found the china clay workings around its summit weirdly beautiful, but perhaps that's just my interest in mining, quarrying and industrial archaeology – an interest spawned solely through my walking.

I must not omit watching the Red Arrows aerobatic display above Eastbourne from Willingdon Hill (visited on the Wilmington Hill route, Section 4) – talk about a ringside seat for free! Then there is the time I lay down to look over the overhanging cliff in Cheddar Gorge, which is mentioned as an option on the Beacon Batch route (Section 2). For those with nerves of steel, this must be one of the finest views from any of the walks in this book even if it did give me the feeling that the whole thing was about to crumble away at any second.

One of my favourite scenes was watching the sun set over the Isle of Portland from Swyre Head (Section 3). First the sky turned pink and that was then followed by the sea before all became laced with lilac clouds. It did, however, occur to me at that point that the torch I had left in the car might come in quite useful on the descent! It's only when a whole flock of sheep turned and looked at me in a puzzled sort of way that it occurred to me that I might be completely mad. Never mind, though, that was one of those experiences that I would not have missed for the world.

I hope that all those who follow my routes can also take away with them experiences like mine. That is what hillwalking is all about. It is not just another form of exercise but much, much more. In the right time and the right place, it can even help you put the rest of your life in some sort of perspective, and that is a supreme gift.

The Hill Names and their Meanings

The knowledge of the meaning of a hill name gives a fascinating insight into not only the topography of the hill but to how our ancestors saw it and used it. The gorse bushes on Win Green have long since disappeared and the post that gave Staple Hill its name may have been lost to history but there is still a fort on Walbury Hill and many people may be curious as to why Leith Hill is so called and what caused somebody to give Dundry Down its name. This section is intended to answer those questions and has been simplified greatly to give the information in a concise and clear way without giving all the evidence that the experts have used to come to their decisions.

Each hill name is given a translation and the words and languages from which its name originates. These place-name elements are given in the order of the original name. The following abbreviations have been used to show the languages from which the elements originate:

OE   Old English (c.450 – c.1100)
ME   Middle English (c.1100 – c.1500)
Eng   Modern English (c.1500 – present)
PrW   Pre-Welsh
Wel   Welsh
Co   Cornish

Again, the Ordnance Survey spellings have been used as the standard modern form of the name, which is not necessarily the one used locally.

Where appropriate, an older name has also been given where the modern name has changed beyond recognition from the original.

The Names and their Meanings

The number in brackets after the name is the section in which that hill lies.

Beacon Batch (2) – signal-fire or lookout point of the valley, ME *bache*.

Black Down (4) – black hill, OE *dun*.

Botley Hill (4) – hill of Botta's clearing, OE personal name + OE *leah*.

Bredon Hill (5) – the hill called 'Bre', OE *dun*. In fact, the first element, bre, derives from PrW *brez*, meaning hill. Thus, the name derives from three words meaning hill from successive languages.

Brighstone Down (3) – the hill of the farmstead of a man called Beorhtwig, OE personal name + OE *tun* + OE *dun*.

Brown Willy (1) – hill of swallows, Co *bron* + Co *guennol*.

Butser Hill (4) – hill of Briht's slope, OE personal name + OE *ora*.

Carnmenellis (1) – stacked tor or rock-pile, Co *carn* + Co *manal*.

Castle Hill (4) – self-explanatory Eng name in reference to the ancient castle above Thurnham.

Chanctonbury Hill (4) – hill of the earthwork of the farmstead near a brushwood thicket, OE *saengel* + OE *tun* + OE *burh*.

Cheriton Hill (4) – the hill of the village with a church, OE *cirice* + OE *tun*.

Christ Cross (2) – the self-explanatory name of the nearby road junction.

Cleeve Hill (5) – hill of the cliff, OE *clif*, in reference to the limestone crag of Cleeve Cloud on the western escarpment, previously called Wendlesclif (AD 780), which is thought to be the cliff of Wendel, who may be a mythological character.

Cliffe Hill (4) – hill of the cliff or steep escarpment, OE *clif*.

Crowborough (4) – hill frequented by crows, OE *crawe* + OE *beorg*.

Ditchling Beacon (4) – signal fire or look-out point of the village of Ditchling, the settlement of the family of a man called Dicel, OE personal name.

Dundry Down (2) – the hill of the slope used for dragging down loads, OE *dun* + OE *draeg* + OE *dun*.

Dunkery Beacon (2) – meaning uncertain but *Dunkery* is derived from Co *dun*, meaning hill fort.

Firle Beacon (4) – signal fire or look-out point of the village of Firle, the place where oak trees grow, OE *fierel*.

Hardown Hill (3) – grey hill, OE *har* + OE *dun*.

Hensbarrow Beacon (1) – possibly signal fire or look-out point at the barrow on the moor where wild birds live, OE *henn*.

Kit Hill (1) – meaning uncertain. *Kit* may simply mean hill.

Leith Hill (4) – hill of the curving escarpment, OE *hlith*.

Lewesdon Hill (3) – possibly hill of Leof's farm, OE personal name + OE *tun*.

Long Knoll (3) – the long hill that is small in extent, Eng derivation.

Nine Barrow Down (3) – the hill of the nine burial mounds, OE *dun*.

Periton Hill (2) – meaning uncertain, possibly hill of the farm of the pear tree, OE *pirige* + OE *tun*.

Selworthy Beacon (2) – signal fire or lookout point of the village of Selworthy, the enclosure by a copse of willow trees, OE *sele* + OE *wothig*.

St Boniface Down (3) – the hill of Saint Boniface, OE *dun*.

Staple Hill (2) – hill of the pillar or post, OE *stapol*.

Swyre Head (3) – the end point of a neck of land, OE *sweora*.

Walbury Hill (3) – hill of the fort of the British, OE *walth* + OE *burh*.

Watch Croft (1) – meaning uncertain. The summit is part of the upland with the self-explanatory name White Downs.

Wendover Woods (4) – the woods of the town of Wendover. The town takes its name from a stream with a Celtic river name meaning 'white waters'.

Wills Neck (2) – meaning uncertain. *Wills* may mean spring, OE *will*.

Wilmington Hill (4) – hill of the estate associated with a man called Wighelm, OE personal name + OE *ing* + OE *tun*.

Win Green (3) – known as *Wingreen Hill* (1812) – hill of the green gorse or patch of gorse, Wel *chwyn*.

Personal Log

Section 1 – The Cornish Hills

NAME	HEIGHT	GRID REFERENCE	DATE OF FIRST ASCENT
Brown Willy	420m / 1377ft	SX 158800	
Kit Hill	334m / 1096ft	SX 375713	
Hensbarrow Beacon	312m / 1025ft	SW 997575	
Carnmenellis	252m / 828ft	SW 696364	
Watch Croft	252m / 828ft	SW 420357	

Section 2 – The Somerset Hills and West Devon

NAME	HEIGHT	GRID REFERENCE	DATE OF FIRST ASCENT
Dunkery Beacon	519m / 1704ft	SS 891416	
Wills Neck	384m / 1261ft	ST 165352	
Beacon Batch	325m / 1066ft	ST 484572	
Staple Hill	315m / 1035ft	ST 240167	
Selworthy Beacon	308m / 1012ft	SS 919480	
Periton Hill	297m / 973ft	SS 946442	
Christ Cross	261m / 857ft	SS 964052	
Dundry Down	233m / 764ft	ST 553667	

Section 3 – The Wessex Downs and the Isle of Wight

NAME	HEIGHT	GRID REFERENCE	DATE OF FIRST ASCENT
Walbury Hill	297m / 974ft	SU 373616	
Long Knoll	288m / 945ft	ST 786376	
Lewesdon Hill	279m / 915ft	ST 437012	

Win Green	277m / 910ft	ST 925206
St Boniface Down	240m / 786ft	SZ 568785
Brighstone Down	214m / 701ft	SZ 432847
Swyre Head	208m / 682ft	SY 934784
Hardown Hill	207m / 678ft	SY 405942
Nine Barrow Down	199m / 653ft	SZ 008811

Section 4 – South-east England

NAME	HEIGHT	GRID REFERENCE	DATE OF FIRST ASCENT
Leith Hill	295m / 968ft	TQ 139431	
Black Down	280m / 919ft	SU 919296	
Butser Hill	270m / 887ft	SU 717203	
Wendover Woods	267m / 876ft	SP 890089	
Botley Hill	267m / 875ft	TQ 396553	
Ditchling Beacon	248m / 813ft	TQ 331130	
Crowborough	242m / 794ft	TQ 510305	
Chanctonbury Hill	238m / 782ft	TQ 134120	
Firle Beacon	217m / 713ft	TQ 485059	
Wilmington Hill	214m / 702ft	TQ 548034	
Castle Hill	200m / 656ft	TQ 804586	
Cheriton Hill	188m / 617ft	TR 197396	
Cliffe Hill	164m / 538ft	TQ 434107	

Section 5 – The Cotswolds

NAME	HEIGHT	GRID REFERENCE	DATE OF FIRST ASCENT
Cleeve Hill	330m / 1083ft	SO 997246	
Bredon Hill	299m / 980ft	SO 958402	

SECTION		TOTAL	DONE
1	The Cornish Hills	05	
2	The Somerset Hills and West Devon	08	
3	The Wessex Downs and the Isle of Wight	09	
4	South-east England	13	
5	The Cotswolds	02	
	Total	37	

Glossary

Absolute height The height of a summit above mean sea level, cf. *relative height*.

Anticline A type of fold in rock formations resembling an n-shape, cf. *syncline*.

Bagger A hillwalker who sets about climbing all the summits of a given type that are on a certain list. Hardened summit baggers give little consideration to climbing an interesting route but rather tackle the shortest route so that they may climb several summits in one day.

Bridleway A right of way on which horses, cyclists and walkers are legally permitted to travel, cf. *byway, footpath, path* and *track*.

Byway A right of way on which all modes of transport are legally permitted to travel, cf. *bridleway, footpath* and *track*.

Carboniferous See geological timescale (page 66).

Cassiterite Tin oxide (SnO_2). The main ore of Cornish tin.

Chalk Calcium carbonate ($CaCO_3$). A very pure form of limestone found in southern and eastern England (see Section 3).

Charcoal A rich source of carbon derived from wood heated in the absence of air. Charcoal was used as a form of carbon in some mineral smelting processes.

China Clay A white powder formed from the decomposition of granitic feldspars, kaolinite being a major constituent. Also known as kaolin (see Section 1).

Coal A deposit consisting of the compacted remains of plants that grew in tropical swamps.

Concave A hillside curved like the interior of a saucer, cf. *convex*.

Conglomerate A rock containing stones and pebbles, cemented together by finer material.

Convex A hillside curved like the exterior of an upturned saucer, cf. *concave*.

Cretaceous See geological timescale (page 66).

Cuesta A ridge that has a cross-sectional profile of a gentle rise, *dipslope*, on one side and a steep *escarpment* on the other side.

Dawson's tables A list compiled by Alan Dawson of a group of hills called *Marilyns*.

Deltaic Of or relating to a delta or estuary at the mouth of a river.

Devonian See geological timescale (page 66).

Dewpond An artificial hollow constructed for the collection of condensed water from mist as a source of drinking water for stock in otherwise waterless land.

Dipslope A gentle slope rising with the strike or strata of the rock to culminate at the top of the *escarpment*. The whole ridge is known as a *cuesta*.

Escarpment A steep and/or precipitous hillslope, often combined with a *dipslope* to form a *cuesta*.

Fault The boundary between divisions of the earth's crust, or upper layer, that breaks the continuity of the rock *strata*.

Flints A glass-like stone found with *chalk* that is formed from the skeletons of sea sponges.

Footpath A right of way along which only pedestrians are legally permitted to travel, cf. *bridleway*, *byway* and *path*. A footpath may not always be visible on the ground.

Fossil The impression of a dead marine creature that has since decomposed or a skeleton/bone left behind in the rock.

Galena Lead sulphide (PbS). The main form of lead ore that was mined in the Mendips (Section 2).

Granite A coarsely grained *igneous* rock, mainly consisting of the minerals mica, quartz and feldspar.

Gritstone A coarse grained *sedimentary* rock deposited generally on beaches and in deserts. See also *sandstone*.

Haematite Iron oxide (Fe_2O_3). The most important iron ore (see Section 4). See also *ironstone*.

Ice Age The last period of extreme coldness in the earth's climate, in which Britain underwent extensive glaciation.

Igneous rocks A rock formed from molten magma either on the surface or underground as an intrusion.

Ironstone A rock, usually either a mudstone or limestone, with a high iron content, usually due to production of iron oxides by colonies of bacteria. See also *haematite*.

Jurassic See geological timescale (page 66).

Lias An alternating sequence of clays and limestones forming the lowest group of rocks deposited in the *Jurassic* succession.

Limestone A crystalline and bedded form of calcium carbonate ($CaCO_3$) that is broken by bedding planes and vertical joints. See also *chalk, ironstone, lias* and *oolitic limestone*.

Marilyn A hill in Britain that rises 492ft (150m) relative to its surroundings.

Mountain building episode See *orogeny*.

Mudstone A *sedimentary rock* formed from compaction of mud in marine or fresh water conditions. See also *shale*.

Munro A Scottish hill above 3,000ft (914m) as defined in 'Munro's Tables' (published by the Scottish Mountaineering Club).

Old Red Sandstone Continent A landmass formed in the Devonian period due to the erosion of the Caledonian fold mountains.

Oolitic limestone A type of *Jurassic* limestone that is made up of tiny nodules, known as oolites (see Section 5). See also *limestone*.

Orogeny A period of mountain building. This is generally due to tectonic activity that results in the construction of fold mountains at or near to a collision boundary (see Geological Introduction).

Path Used in this book to define a strip of ground eroded by the passage of feet, which is too narrow to drive an all-terrain vehicle along, cf. *bridleway, footpath* and *track*.

Peat Undecomposed plant remains forming a black soil.

Permian See geological timescale (page 66).

Pillbox A small enclosed concrete fort dating from the Second World War.

Relative height The height of a summit relative to its surrounding landscape, rather than to sea level, cf. *absolute height*.

Sandstone A sedimentary rock formed by compression of sand on beaches or in deserts. See also *gritstone*.

Scarp See *escarpment*.

Sedimentary rocks A rock formed from the compression of sediments on land or under water.

Shale A *sedimentary* rock formed from fine particles. See also *mudstone*.

Strata Layers in rocks.

Strip lynchets Ancient field boundaries in the form of level areas separated by banks running across the slope.

Syncline A U-shaped fold in a series of rocks, cf. *anticline.*

Tertiary See geological timescale (page 66).

Tor A rocky peak or summit, particularly on the moorlands of the south-west (Section 1).

Track Used in this guide to refer to a strip of ground eroded by either feet or vehicles so that it is wide enough to drive an all-terrain vehicle along, cf. *bridleway, byway, footpath* and *path.*

Triassic See geological timescale (page 66).

Trigonometric point A concrete pillar constructed by the Ordnance Survey to conduct trigonometrical surveys. Often abbreviated to trig point.

Unconformity A break in rock strata that indicates that no new rocks were deposited for a certain period of time.

Wind chill The cold feeling caused by the wind. This is a particular problem when the north or east wind blows in winter across the hills of southern England.

Further Reading

In the same series

Dibb, Alasdair, *England's Highest Peaks: A Guide to the 2,000ft Summits* (Mainstream Publishing, 2000)
Dibb, Alasdair, *The Hills of England: A Guide to the Summits Below 2,000ft*:
   Volume 1: *Southern England* (Mainstream Publishing, 2002)
   Volume 2: *The Midlands and South Pennines* (Mainstream Publishing, 2002)
   Volume 3: *Northern England and the Isle of Man* (Mainstream Publishing, 2002)

Lists

Dawson, Alan, *The Relative Hills of Britain* (Cicerone Press, 1992) (Amended by subsequent update sheets, up to and including 1999.)

Section 1

Brooks, John, *Pathfinder Guide 5: Cornwall Walks* (Jarrold Publishing, 2000)
Thompson, E.V. (ed), *Walks on Bodmin Moor* (Bossiney Books, 1996)
100 Walks in Devon and Cornwall (The Crowood Press, 1996)

Section 2

Atkin, Brian, *Exmoor's Greatest Walks* (Exmoor Books, 2000)

Atkin, Brian, *Exmoor Walks from Minehead* (Exmoor Books, 1998)

Conduit, Brian, *Pathfinder Guide 1: South Devon and Dartmoor Walks* (Jarrold Publishing, 1998)

Conduit, Brian, *Pathfinder Guide 9: Exmoor and the Quantocks Walks* (Jarrold Publishing, 1999)

Conduit, Brian, *Pathfinder Guide 21: Somerset, Wiltshire and the Mendips Walks* (Jarrold Publishing, 1997)

Farrant, A.R., *Walks Around the Caves and Karst of the Mendip Hills* (British Cave Research Association, 1999)

Macadam, John, *Recreational Path Guide: The Two Moors Way* (Aurum Press, 1997)

Main, Laurence, *Walks in Mysterious Somerset* (Sigma Leisure, 1999)

Stoker, Hugh, *East Devon Walks* (Mill House Publications, 1984)

Vile, Nigel, *Family Walks in Mendip, Avalon and Sedgemoor* (Scarthin Books, 1991)

100 Walks in Devon and Cornwall (The Crowood Press, 1996)

Section 3

Bowness, Timothy and Mitchell, Douglas (eds), *100 Walks in Hampshire and Isle of Wight* (The Crowood Press, 1994)

Burton, Anthony, *Recreational Path Guide: Wessex Ridgeway* (Aurum Press, 1999)

Conduit, Brian, *Pathfinder Guide 11: Dorset Walks* (Jarrold Publishing, 1999)

Curtis, Neil, *National Trail Guide: The Ridgeway* (Aurum Press, 1999)

Edwards, Anne-Marie, *Pathfinder Guide: Isle of Wight Walks* (Jarrold Publishing, 1994)

Griffiths, Edward R., *More Circular Dorset Walks* (Green Fields Books, 2000)

Legg, Rodney, *Purbeck Coastal Walks* (Dorset Publishing Company, 1994)

Legg, Rodney, *Walks in West Dorset* (Dorset Publishing Company, 1986)

Main, Laurence, *Walks in Mysterious Wiltshire* (Sigma Leisure, 1998)

Plucknett, Jenny, *Pathfinder Guide 12: Hampshire and New Forest Walks* (Jarrold Publishing, 2001)

Sale, Richard (ed), *100 Walks in Dorset* (The Crowood Press, 1995)

Stoker, Hugh, *South Dorset Walks* (Mill House Publications, 1983)
Stoker, Hugh, *Wildtrack Walks in West Dorset* (Mill House Publications, 1996)
100 Walks in Oxon and Berkshire (The Crowood Press, 1997)
100 Walks in Wiltshire (The Crowood Press, 1997)

Section 4

Bowness, Timothy and Mitchell, Douglas (eds), *100 Walks in Hampshire and Isle of Wight* (The Crowood Press, 1994)
Brooks, John, *Pathfinder Guide 8: Kent Walks* (Jarrold Publishing, 1996)
Brooks, John and Conduit, Brian, *Pathfinder Guide 24: Surrey and Sussex Walks* (Jarrold Publishing, 2000)
Conduit, Brian, *Pathfinder Guide 25: Chilterns and Thames Valley Walks* (Jarrold Publishing, 1997)
Conduit, Brian, *Pathfinder Guide 37: In and Around London Walks* (Jarrold Publishing, 1999)
Conduit, Brian, *Pathfinder Guide: More Cotswold Walks* (Jarrold Publishing, 2000)
Curtis, Neil, *National Trail Guide: The Ridgeway* (Aurum Press, 1999)
Curtis, Neil and Walker, Jim, *National Trail Guide: The North Downs Way* (Aurum Press, 2000)
Haine, Angela and Owen, Susan, *Discovering Walks in Surrey* (Shire Publications Ltd., 1995)
Harrison, D., *Exploring Brighton and the South Downs* (SB Publications, 1996)
Harrison, D., *Exploring Eastbourne and the South Downs* (SB Publications, 1995)
Hatts, Leigh, *25 Walks: the Chilterns* (The Mercat Press, 1997)
Hinson, Donald J., *50 Hill Walks in the Chilterns* (Sigma Leisure, 1998)
Jenner, Lorna et al., *Along and Around the High Weald Landscape Trail* (High Weald Forum, 1999)
Knowlton, Derrick, *Walks in Hampshire* (Frederick Warne, 1985)
Krynski, Audrey and Spayne, Janet, *Walks in the Kent Hills* (Countryside Books, 2000)
Krynski, Audrey and Spayne, Janet, *Walks in the Surrey Hills* (Countryside Books, 1991)
McCloy, Andrew, *Walks with Children in the Surrey Hills* (Questa Publishing, 1995)

Millmore, Paul et al., *National Trail Guide: The South Downs Way* (Aurum Press, 1996)

Moon, Nick, *Family Walks: Chilterns North* (The Book Castle, 1998)

Moon, Nick, *Family Walks: Chilterns South* (The Book Castle, 1997)

Palmer, Derek, *Walks in East Sussex* (Countryside Books, 1994)

Plucknett, Jenny, *Pathfinder Guide 12: Hampshire and New Forest Walks* (Jarrold Publishing, 2001)

Reynolds, Kev, *The Wealdway and the Vanguard Way* (Cicerone Press, 1987)

Roberts, Liz, *Walks in the Chilterns* (Countryside Books, 1990)

Sale, Richard, *100 Walks in Surrey* (The Crowood Press, 1994)

Sale, Richard (ed), *100 Walks in West Sussex* (The Crowood Press, 1995)

Sale, Richard (ed), *100 Walks in East Sussex* (The Crowood Press, 1994)

Sale, Richard (ed), *100 Walks in Kent* (The Crowood Press, 1995)

Woodcock, Roy, *Best Walks in the Chilterns* (Constable, 1998)

Wright, Christopher John, *A Guide to the Pilgrim's Way and North Downs Way* (Constable, 1993)

Section 5

Brooks, John and Conduit, Brian, *Pathfinder Guide 6: Cotswold Walks* (Jarrold Publishing, 2000)

Burton, Anthony, *Recreational Path Guide: the Cotswold Way* (Aurum Press, 1995)

Conduit, Brian, *Pathfinder Guide 21: Somerset, Wiltshire and the Mendips Walks* (Jarrold Publishing, 1997)

Fryer, B.E., *25 Walks: The Cotswolds* (The Mercat Press, 1996)

Holmes, Clive, *Cotswolds Walks:*
  Book 1: North (Cicerone Press, 1993)
  Book 2: Central (Cicerone Press, 1993)
  Book 3: South (Cicerone Press, 1993)

Kershaw, Ronald and Robson, Brian, *Discovering Walks in the Cotswolds* (Shire Publications Ltd., 1989)

Meech, Julie, *Discovering Walks in the Cotswolds* (Sigma Leisure, 1998)

Moon, Nick, *Oxfordshire Walks: Oxford, the Cotswolds and the Cherwell Valley* (The Book Castle, 1998)

Geology

Toghill, Peter, *The Geology of Britain: An Introduction* (Swan Hill Press, 2000)
Whittow, John, *Geology and Scenery in Britain* (Chapman and Hall, 1992)

Place-names

Cameron, K. (ed), *The Place-names of Berkshire* (The English Place-name Society, 1974)
Coates, Richard, *Hampshire Place-Names* (Ensign Publications, 1993)
Ekwall, Eilert, *The Concise Oxford Dictionary of English Place-Names*, 4th edition (Oxford at the Clarendon Press, 1960)
Fägerstein, Anton, *The Place Names of Dorset* (EP Publishing Ltd., 1978)
Gelling, Margaret, *Place-Names in the Landscape* (J.M. Dent Ltd., 1993)
Gover, J.E.B., Mawer, A. and Stenton, F.M., *The Place-Names of Surrey* (Cambridge at the University Press, 1934)
Longstaff, John C., *Notes on Wiltshire Names: Vol 1 – Place-Names* (W.M. Dotesio, The Library Press, 1911)
Mawer, A. and Stention, F.M., *The Place-Names of Sussex* (Cambridge at the University Press, 1930)
Mills, A.D., *A Dictionary of English Place-Names* (Oxford University Press, 1991)
Padel, O.J., *Cornish Place-Name Elements* (English Place-Name Society, 1985)

Other

Davies, Barry, *Collins Gem Hillwalker's Survival Guide* (HarperCollins, 1999)
Graydon, Don and Hanson, Kurt (eds), *Mountaineering: The Freedom of the Hills* (Swan Hill Press, 1997)
Sharp, D.W.A., *The Penguin Dictionary of Chemistry* (Penguin Books, 1990)
The YHA Guide 2001 (Youth Hostels Association, 2000)
Uvarov, E.B. and Isaacs, Alan, *The Penguin Dictionary of Science* (Penguin Books, 1993).

Useful Telephone Numbers

Several places and attractions are mentioned in the main part of the book but telephone numbers are not given to avoid breaking up the text. Instead, they are given here along with other useful numbers for tourist information centres and national park centres. It should also be noted that some attractions and information centres are closed during the winter months although generally those in and around large towns are more likely to remain open.

General

National Rail Enquiry Service (Advanced Timetable and Fare Information, 24hr service) – 08457 484950

Section I – The Cornish Hills

Youth Hostels (YHA) –
    Boscastle Harbour (01840) 250287. For bookings more than seven
        days in advance call (01629) 592707.
    Boswinger (01726) 843234
    Coverack (01326) 280687
    Elmscott (01237) 441367. For bookings more than seven days in
        advance call (01629) 592707.
    Golant (01726) 833507
    Land's End (01736) 788437
    Penzance (01736) 362666
    Perranporth (01872) 573812
    Plymouth (01752) 562189
    Tintagel (01840) 770334
    Treyarnon Bay (01841) 520322

Tourist Information Centres –
Bodmin (01208) 76616
Bude (01288) 354240
Camelford (01840) 212954
Fowey (01726) 833616
Helston & Lizard Peninsula (01326) 565431
Ilfracombe (01271) 863001
Launceston (01566) 772321
Looe (01503) 262072
Newquay (01637) 854020
Padstow (01841) 533449
Penzance (01736) 632207
Plymouth (01752) 304849
St Ives (01736) 796297
Tavistock (01822) 612938
Truro (01872) 274555
Wadebridge (01208) 813725

Section 2 – The Somerset Hills and West Devon

Cheddar Showcaves (01934) 742343
Exmoor National Park Centres –
Combe Martin (01271) 883319
County Gate (01598) 741321
Dulverton (01398) 323841
Dunster (01643) 821835
Lynmouth (01598) 752509
Porlock (01643) 863150
Wookey Hole Caves (01749) 672243

Youth Hostels (YHA) –
Bath (01225) 465674
Beer (01297) 20296
Bristol (0117) 9221659
Cheddar (01934) 742494
Dartington (01803) 862303
Exeter (01392) 873329
Exford (01643) 831288

Ilfracombe (01271) 865337
Lynton (01598) 753237
Maypool (01803) 842444
Minehead (01643) 702595
Okehampton (01837) 53916
Plymouth (01752) 562189
Quantock Hills (01278) 741224. For bookings more than seven days
    in advance call (01629) 592707.
Salcombe (01458) 842856
Steps Bridge (01647) 252435. For bookings more than seven days in
    advance call (01629) 592707.
Street (01458) 442961

Tourist Information Centres –
  Axminster (01297) 34386
  Barnstaple (01271) 375000
  Bath (01225) 477101
  Bideford (01237) 477676
  Bradford-on-Avon (01225) 865797
  Bridgwater (01278) 427652
  Bristol (0117) 9260767
  Burnham-on-Sea (01278) 787852
  Chard (01460) 67463
  Cheddar (01934) 744071
  Crediton (01363) 772006
  Dartmouth (01803) 834224
  Exeter (01392) 265700
  Glastonbury (01458) 832954
  Lynton (01598) 752225
  Minehead (01643) 702624
  Paignton (0906) 6801268
  Plymouth (01752) 304849
  Seaton (01297) 21660
  Shepton Mallet (01749) 345258
  Sidmouth (01395) 516441
  South Molton (01769) 574122
  Taunton (01823) 336344
  Tavistock (01822) 612938
  Tiverton (01884) 255827
  Torquay (0906) 6808268
  Torrington (01805) 626140

Totnes (01803) 863168
Wells (01749) 672552
Weston-Super-Mare (01934) 888800

Section 3 – The Wessex Downs and the Isle of Wight

Youth Hostels (YHA) –
  Beer (01297) 20296
  Burley (01425) 403233
  Litton Cheney (01308) 482340. For bookings more than seven days in
      advance call (01629) 592707.
  Lulworth Cove (01929) 400564
  Portland (01305) 861368
  Portsmouth (0239) 2375661
  Salisbury (01722) 327572
  Sandown (01983) 402651
  Streatley-on-Thames (01491) 872278
  Swanage (01929) 422113
  The Ridgeway (01235) 760253
  Totland Bay (01983) 752165
  Winchester (01962) 853723

Tourist Information Centres –
  Amesbury (01980) 622833
  Andover (01264) 324320
  Avebury (01672) 539425
  Axminster (01297) 34386
  Basingstoke (01256) 817618
  Blandford Forum (01258) 454770
  Bournemouth (0906) 8020234 – calls cost 50p per minute
  Bradford-on-Avon (01225) 865797
  Bridport (01308) 424901
  Chard (01460) 67463
  Chippenham (01249) 706333
  Christchurch (01202) 471780
  Cowes (01983) 291914
  Devizes (01380) 729408
  Dorchester (01305) 267992

Frome (01373) 467271
Lyme Regis (01297) 442138
Marlborough (01672) 513989
Mere (01747) 861211
Newbury (01635) 30267
Poole (01202) 253253
Portsmouth (02392) 826722
Reading (0118) 9566226
Ryde (01983) 562905
Salisbury (01722) 334956
Sandown (01983) 403886
Seaton (01297) 21660
Shaftesbury (01747) 853514
Shanklin (01983) 862942
Sherborne (01935) 815341
Sidmouth (01395) 516441
Swanage (01929) 422885
Trowbridge (01225) 777054
Ventnor (01983) 853625
Warminster (01985) 218548
Westbury (01373) 827158
Weymouth (01305) 785747
Wimborne Minster (01202) 886116
Winchester (01962) 840500
Yarmouth (01983) 760015
Yeovil (01935) 471279

Section 4 – South-east England

Youth Hostels (YHA) –
    Alfriston (01323) 870423
    Blackboys (01825) 890607
    Bradenham (01494) 562929. To make a booking call (01895) 673188.
    Brighton (01273) 556196
    Broadstairs (01843) 604121
    Canterbury (01227) 462911
    Dover (01304) 201314
    Eastbourne (01323) 721081

Hastings (01424) 812373
Hindhead (01428) 604285. For bookings more than seven days in advance call (01629) 592707.
Holmbury St Mary (01306) 730777
Jordans (01494) 873135
Kemsing (01732) 761341
Margate (01843) 221616
Medway (01634) 400788
Portsmouth (0239) 2375661
Tanners Hatch (01306) 877964
Telscombe (01273) 301357. For bookings more than seven days in advance call (01629) 592707.
Truleigh Hill (01903) 813419
Windsor (01753) 861710

Tourist Information Centres –
Arundel (01903) 882268
Ashford (01233) 629165
Aylesbury (01296) 330559
Battle (01424) 773721
Bexhill-on-Sea (01424) 732208
Bognor Regis (01243) 823140
Brighton (0906) 7112255 – calls cost 50p per minute
Canterbury (01227) 766567
Chichester (01243) 775888
Dover (01304) 205108
Eastbourne (01323) 411400
Folkestone (01303) 258594
Guildford (01483) 444333
Hastings (01424) 781111
Henley-on-Thames (01491) 578034
High Wycombe (01494) 421892
Hythe (01303) 267799
Lewes (01273) 483448
Littlehampton (01903) 713480
Maidstone (01622) 602169
Midhurst (01730) 817322
Petersfield (01730) 268829
Petworth (01798) 343523
Portsmouth (02392) 826722
Reading (0118) 9566226

Rochester (01634) 843666
Rye (01797) 226696
Seaford (01323) 897426
Tenterden (01580) 763572
Tonbridge (01732) 770929
Tunbridge Wells (01892) 515675
Wendover (01296) 696759
Winchester (01962) 840500
Worthing (01903) 210022

Section 5 – The Cotswolds

Youth Hostels (YHA) –
  Charlbury (01608) 810202
  Duntisbourne (01285) 821682
  Oxford (01865) 762997
  Oxford (Botley Road) (01865) 727275
  Stow-on-the-Wold (01451) 830497
  The Ridgeway (01235) 760253
Tourist Information Centres –
  Burford (01993) 823558
  Cheltenham (01242) 522878
  Cherwell Valley (01869) 345888
  Chipping Norton (01608) 644379
  Didcot (01235) 813243
  Evesham (01386) 446944
  Faringdon (01367) 242191
  Gloucester (01452) 421188
  Oxford (01865) 726871
  Pershore (01386) 554262
  Stow-on-the-Wold (01451) 831082
  Stroud (01453) 765768
  Tewkesbury (01684) 295027
  Upton upon Severn (01684) 594200
  Winchcombe (01242) 602925

Index to the Series

This index covers all the separate hills and mountains of England that are covered in the three volumes of *The Hills of England* series and *England's Highest Peaks*. Each summit is referenced to the book(s) in which it appears, although page references are not given. **EHP** refers to *England's Highest Peaks*, **Vol 1**, **Vol 2** and **Vol 3** refer to Volumes 1 (*Southern England*), 2 (*The Midlands and South Pennines*) and 3 (*Northern England and the Isle of Man*) of *The Hills of England* series. **Sec** refers to the section in which that particular summit is primarily described.